Essentials of Cerebral Palsy Football

Essentials of Cerebral Palsy Football introduces the reader to the practice of Cerebral Palsy (CP) football. This is a worldwide 7-a-side style of football played by people with CP and acquired brain injuries. CP football is played across the world in over seventy countries covering six continents and is governed by the International Federation of CP Football (IFCPF) and a multitude of regional federations responsible for promoting, managing and governing CP football.

This book examines the current research and findings and provides an understanding of the history of CP football, the basics of CP and eligible impairments, game rules and regulations and current scientific knowledge regarding the sport's performance. Special emphasis is given to providing CP football coaches and professionals with relevant information to apply in the practical field.

Essentials of Cerebral Palsy Football provides a practical, hands-on guide for the CP football community based on the current status of scientific research related to this team Para sport development and performance. It also seeks to provide students instruction into the different areas of disability in a high-level sports environment and understanding how professionals from different fields can contribute to the improvement and professionalisation of the different areas of sports performance and development.

This cutting-edge book is key reading for the CP football community including people registered in CP sports or football federations, Para sport stakeholders, coaches, conditioning coaches, physiotherapists, nutritionists, medical staff and practitioners.

Iván Peña-González, PhD, is a Lecturer in the Department of Sport Sciences at the Miguel Hernandez University of Elche, UMH, Spain, and a Researcher in the GIAFIS research group at the Sport Research Centre of the same university. His research is focused on physical performance in football. He has done specific research about the physical performance demands, talent identification and international selection processes in CP football. He is the Head of the Sports Research Department of the Spanish Federation of CP Sports (FEDPC). He has collaborated with the FEDPC as a physical-conditioning coach in the Spanish CP football National Team for five years, including the U19 and Absolute teams. He achieved a silver medal in the U19 World Cup and a bronze medal in an Absolute European Championship.

Raúl Reina, PhD, is a Full Professor of Adapted Physical Activity and Para sports in the Bachelor's on Physical Activity and Sport Sciences and in Occupational Therapy at UMH, Spain. He is a Researcher at the Sports Research Centre of the UMH and a Member of the research group on motor control and learning. His main research interest is focused on classification in Para sports to explore the relationships between physical impairments and activity limitation when performing sports skills to develop evidence-based and sport-specific classification systems. He is also the Classification Director of the IFCPF and International Classifier for World Para Athletics (former IPC Athletics) and World Boccia and the Director of the Classification Commission of the Spanish Paralympic Committee.

Manuel Moya-Ramón, PhD, is a Full Professor in the Department of Sport Sciences at the UMH, Spain, with extensive experience in research regarding training periodisation, training load monitoring and quantification, and physical performance assessment in sports and CP football. He is also the Director of the Sports Training Analysis and Optimization Laboratory, one of the four laboratories in the Sports Research Centre of the UMH, and the Head of the GIAFIS research group.

As President of the International Federation of Cerebral Palsy Football (IFCPF), it is an honour and a privilege to extend my endorsement to this work, which captures the essence and evolution of our sport.

Football for individuals with cerebral palsy represents not only high-level athletic competition but also a testament to resilience, effort, and passion. This book, through its detailed narrative and commitment to inclusion, reflects these fundamental values that we promote in each of our events and competitions.

The research and dedication poured into these pages not only highlight the physical, technical and tactical aspects of CP football but also celebrate the inspiring stories of our female and male players, coaches, and communities around the world. This is an invaluable resource for both enthusiasts of the sport and those seeking to understand and support the inclusive movement within the sporting realm, as well as for the coaches and technicians who professionally dedicate themselves to CP football.

On behalf of the IFCPF, I express my deepest gratitude to the author for their significant contribution to the recognition and dissemination of CP football. I am confident that this work will be a source of inspiration and knowledge that transcends borders and generations.

With the firm conviction that this book will enrich the legacy of our sport, I offer my highest endorsement and recommend it wholeheartedly to all those interested in football and sporting inclusion.

Sincerely,
Jan-Hein Evers
President of the IFCPF

Routledge Focus on Sport, Culture and Society

Routledge Focus on Sport, Culture and Society showcases the latest cutting-edge research in the sociology of sport and exercise. Concise in form (20,000-50,000 words) and published quickly (within three months), the books in this series represents an important channel through which authors can disseminate their research swiftly and make an impact on current debates. We welcome submissions on any topic within the socio-cultural study of sport and exercise, including but not limited to subjects such as gender, race, sexuality, disability, politics, the media, social theory, Olympic Studies, and the ethics and philosophy of sport. The series aims to be theoretically-informed, empirically-grounded and international in reach, and will include a diversity of methodological approaches.

Available in this series:

Olympic Laws
Culture, Values, Tensions
Mark James and Guy Osborn

Sport and Social Media in Business and Society
Gashaw Abeza and Ryan King-White

Skateboarding and the Senses
Skills, Surfaces, and Spaces
Sander Hölsgens and Brian Glenney

Essentials of Cerebral Palsy Football
Edited by Iván Peña-González, Raúl Reina and Manuel Moya-Ramón

National Symbols at the Olympic Games:
An Olympics Without Flags?
Jörg Krieger

For more information about this series, please visit: https://www.routledge.com/Routledge-Focus-on-Sport-Culture-and-Society/book-series/RFSCS

Essentials of Cerebral Palsy Football

Edited by Iván Peña-González, Raúl Reina and Manuel Moya-Ramón

NEW YORK AND LONDON

First published 2025
by Routledge
605 Third Avenue, New York, NY 10158

and by Routledge
4 Park Square, Milton Park, Abingdon, Oxon, OX14 4RN

Routledge is an imprint of the Taylor & Francis Group, an informa business

ISBN: 9781032708935 (hbk)
ISBN: 9781032708959 (pbk)
ISBN: 9781032708942 (ebk)

DOI: 10.4324/9781032708942

Typeset in Times New Roman
by Deanta Global Publishing Services, Chennai, India

Contents

Foreword

Writing the Foreword for *Essentials of Cerebral Palsy Football* is an honour that fills me with pride and emotion, not only due to my love for the sport but also because of my deep personal and professional connection with football for individuals with cerebral palsy.

I have been fortunate to experience CP football from multiple perspectives: as a player, coach and head of the development of this sport in Spain. My career began as a player in 1995, representing the Spanish National CP Football Team in numerous international competitions. One of the most significant moments of my career was when, alongside my team, we won the bronze medal at the Atlanta 1996 Paralympic Games, an achievement that remains a milestone in my life.

Throughout these years, I have witnessed firsthand the changes and growth of CP football worldwide. New countries have embraced the practice of this Para sport, representation has expanded to all continents, and the integration of women's CP football has become a reality. All these milestones allow CP football to continue growing and gaining international recognition, showcasing this football modality as an increasingly professional Para sport.

As a player, I learned the true meaning of perseverance and dedication. The values derived from my involvement with CP football allowed me to grow athletically, professionally and personally. Every match was an opportunity to demonstrate that, despite adversities, the human spirit is indomitable. My teammates and I competed not only for medals and trophies but also to raise awareness and dignify our Para sport.

After retiring as a player, I took on the role of national coach and head of CP football in Spain, a role I continue to fulfil with immense love and responsibility to this day. In this new stage, I have had the opportunity to give back to the sport a bit of what it has given me. As the national coach, I have enjoyed numerous successes achieved by the team, ensuring that after many years, the Spanish team once again stood on the podium of an international tournament. Working with young players and witnessing firsthand how they develop their talent and passion has been an unparalleled experience.

Essentials of Cerebral Palsy Football is a work that captures the essence and spirit of our sport. From specific tactics and techniques in the professional field to scientific innovations applied to this Para sport, this book is a tribute to all those who have made CP football what it is today. For coaches and technicians, it provides valuable tools and deep knowledge that will enrich their professional practice. For enthusiasts, it offers a window into a world full of inspiring stories and extraordinary achievements.

I hope this book serves as a source of inspiration and knowledge, both for those already involved in CP football and for those discovering this wonderful Para sport for the first time. CP football is not just a sport; it is a community, a family that welcomes everyone with open arms and celebrates every victory, big or small, with the same enthusiasm.

Moreover, the book is not only aimed at athletes, coaches, referees and classifiers, among others, but also at fans, the so-called eighth player, who plays a crucial role in every match, every play, every dispute and every goal scored by the team. I hope this book can open that door for those who are not familiar with CP football and be the first step of many to becoming supporters and accompanying the rest of the community towards common success.

I deeply thank the editors of this book for their dedication and effort in creating this indispensable work. I am confident that, like me, readers will find in these pages a wealth of information and a powerful message of inclusion and resilience.

Jorge Peleteiro Rubio
Former player and head coach of the Spanish National CP Football Team,
Head of CP Football in Spain,
Ibi (Alicante), Spain,
August 2024

Figures

Tables

Contributors

Skye Arthur-Banning
International Federation of CP Football (IFCPF)
Clemson University
South Carolina, United States

Daniel Bueno
Chilean Applied Sport Science Unity
Universidad de Santiago de Chile
Santiago, Chile

Daniel Castillo
Valoración del Rendimiento Deportivo, Actividad Física y Salud y Lesiones Deportivas (REDAFLED)
Faculty of Education
University of Valladolid
Soria, Spain

Eduardo Cervelló
Sport Research Centre, Department of Sports Sciences
Miguel Hernandez University
Elche, Spain

María Isabel Cornejo
Escuela de Kinesiología, Facultad de Salud
Universidad Santo Tomás
Santiago, Chile
Magister en Cs de la Actividad Física y Deporte Aplicadas al Entrenamiento, Rehabilitación y Reintegro Deportivo, Facultad de Salud
Universidad Santo Tomás
Santiago, Chile

Margaret Domka
Clemson University
South Carolina, United States

Tomás García-Calvo
Faculty of Sport Sciences
University of Extremadura
Cáceres, Spain

Matías Henríquez
International Federation of CP Football (IFCPF)
Escuela de Kinesiología, Facultad de Odontología y Ciencias de la Rehabilitación
Universidad San Sebastián
Providencia, Chile

Aitor Iturricastillo
Research Group in Physical Activity, Physical Exercise and Sport (AKTIBOki)
Department of Physical Education and Sport, Faculty of Education and Sport
University of the Basque Country (UPV/EHU)
Vitoria-Gasteiz, Spain
Sports and Physical Exercise Research Group (GIKAFIT)
Department of Physical Education and Sport, Faculty of Education and Sport
University of the Basque Country (UPV/EHU)
Vitoria-Gasteiz, Spain

Heather Jameson
Football Association of Ireland
Ireland Men's CP Football Team
Female CP Football Player
Dublin, Ireland

Alejandro Javaloyes
Sport Research Centre, Department of Sports Sciences
Miguel Hernandez University
Elche, Spain

Kai Lammert
Paralympic National Team (Pararoos) at Football Australia
Sidney, Australia

Tom Langen
International Federation of CP Football (IFCPF)
Nijmegen, the Netherlands

Francisco Leo
Faculty of Sport Sciences
University of Extremadura
Cáceres, Spain

Juan Francisco Maggiolo
Spanish Federation of CP Sports (FEDPC)
River Plate University Institute
Buenos Aires, Argentina
Sport Research Centre, Department of Sports Sciences
Miguel Hernandez University
Elche, Spain

Manuel Moya-Ramón
Sport Research Centre, Department of Sports Sciences
Miguel Hernandez University
Elche, Spain

Iván Peña-González
Spanish Federation of CP Sports (FEDPC)
Sport Research Centre, Department of Sports Sciences
Miguel Hernandez University
Elche, Spain

Raúl Reina
International Federation of CP Football (IFCPF)
Sport Research Centre, Department of Sports Sciences
Miguel Hernandez University
Elche, Spain

Alba Roldan
Sport Research Centre, Department of Sports Sciences
Miguel Hernandez University
Elche, Spain

Jose Manuel Sarabia
Sport Research Centre, Department of Sports Sciences
Miguel Hernandez University
Elche, Spain

Stuart Sharp
US Soccer Federation
Georgia, United States

Sam Turner
International Federation of CP Football (IFCPF)
Para Football Foundation
Lincoln, England

Javier Yanci
Research Group in Physical Activity, Physical Exercise and Sport (AKTIBOki)
Department of Physical Education and Sport, Faculty of Education and Sport
University of the Basque Country (UPV/EHU)
Vitoria-Gasteiz, Spain
Sports and Physical Exercise Research Group (GIKAFIT)
Department of Physical Education and Sport, Faculty of Education and Sport
University of the Basque Country (UPV/EHU)
Vitoria-Gasteiz, Spain

1 Health Conditions Applied to Cerebral Palsy Football

María Isabel Cornejo and Alba Roldan

Contextual Framework

The International Classification of Functioning, Disability, and Health (ICF) is globally acknowledged as a classification system for health and functioning. It serves as a comprehensive and versatile framework, providing a unified and standardised approach to describing and understanding health-related functioning across various contexts, including sports for individuals with disabilities. Developed by the World Health Organization,[1] this regulation encompasses human functioning, addressing not only structural and functional deficiencies but also the broader dimensions of activity limitations and participation restrictions.[2]

This conceptual framework is also employed in categorising sports for individuals with disabilities, enabling the identification of how different health conditions impact the body's structure and function, thereby generating activity limitations and participation restrictions. In the context of this work, participation refers specifically to participation in sport. Consequently, the subsequent chapter will explore the health conditions commonly observed in athletes who participate in football for individuals with CP, elucidating the pertinent structures and functions involved and discussing their implications for specific football-related actions.

Eligible Impairments for CP Football

According to the International Classification Rules and Regulations, the International Federation of Cerebral Palsy Football (IFCPF) provides opportunities for individuals with neurological and/or motor control impairments of a cerebral nature, resulting in permanent and verifiable activity limitations in the performance of fundamental and/or advanced football skills. Eligible impairment types are associated with a range of health conditions, including, but not limited to:

DOI: 10.4324/9781032708942-1

Cerebral Palsy

Cerebral palsy (CP) is a group of conditions with varying degrees of severity, sharing certain developmental characteristics. As described by Rosenbaum et al.,[3] CP is defined as

> a group of permanent disorders of the development of movement and posture, causing activity limitation, that are attributed to non-progressive disturbances that occurred in the developing fetal or infant brain. The motor disorders of CP are often accompanied by disturbances of sensation, perception, cognition, communication, and behaviour, by epilepsy, and by secondary musculoskeletal problems.

CP has multiple aetiologies affecting different parts of the brain, contributing to a broad range of clinical presentations. These aetiological factors can be classified according to the time of brain injury: prenatal, perinatal and postnatal. Prenatal risk factors include multiple gestation, thrombophilia, genetic disorders and intrauterine infections. Perinatal risk factors include asphyxia, instrumental delivery and premature birth. Postnatal risk factors, occurring after childbirth and up to 2 years of age,[4] include periventricular leukomalacia, cerebral infarction, asphyxia and hyperbilirubinemia.[5, 6] These factors were once perceived as direct causes of CP but are now recognised as signs of processes occurring earlier in development. While CP itself is not progressive, the manifestations of the initial brain injury can evolve over a person's life. Thus, it is more accurate to view CP as permanent yet dynamic.

Traumatic Brain Injury

Traumatic brain injury (TBI) occurs when an external force injures the brain. This can result from various incidents such as falls, accidents or blunt trauma to the head. TBIs range from mild (concussions) to severe, causing temporary or permanent neurological damage. Symptoms may include headaches, confusion, memory problems, dizziness and loss of consciousness. TBIs can have profound and long-lasting effects on an individual's physical, cognitive and emotional well-being.[7]

Stroke or Cerebrovascular Accident

A stroke occurs when blood flow to the brain is disrupted, leading to cell death and potential brain damage. This interruption can result from a blocked artery (ischaemic stroke) or a ruptured blood vessel (haemorrhagic stroke). Symptoms include sudden weakness or numbness on one side of the body, difficulty speaking or understanding speech, severe headache, and loss of balance or coordination. Prompt medical attention is crucial to minimise brain damage and prevent complications. Treatment may involve medications, surgical interventions or rehabilitation to aid recovery and prevent recurrence.

The clinical presentation of stroke varies depending on the specific vascular territory affected. For instance, involvement of the anterior cerebral artery may result in hemiparesis with more pronounced involvement of the leg than the arm, gait apraxia and akinetic mutism. Strokes affecting the middle cerebral artery often present with hemiparesis involving the face, arm and leg and may also include aphasia. Vertebrobasilar injuries typically manifest with symptoms such as ataxia and nystagmus. Lacunar stroke syndromes, characterised by occlusion of small penetrating arteries, can lead to either pure motor hemiparesis or ataxic hemiparesis.[8] In addition to these specific manifestations, hemiparesis, muscle weakness and spasticity are commonly observed across various types of strokes.

Friedreich's Ataxia

Friedreich's ataxia (FA) is a rare genetic neurological disorder characterised by progressive damage to the nervous system. It results from mutations in the FXN gene, leading to reduced production of frataxin, a protein vital for mitochondrial function. FA typically manifests in childhood and adolescence, leading to symptoms such as difficulty walking, loss of coordination and balance, muscle weakness, impaired speech and diminished lower limb reflexes. Clinical assessment reveals nose–finger ataxia, upper limb dysdiadochokinesia and impaired heel–shin slide as common early signs. As the condition advances, individuals may experience vision and hearing impairment, scoliosis and cardiomyopathy.[9]

Spinocerebellar Ataxia

Spinocerebellar ataxia (SCA) encompasses a group of inherited neurological disorders characterised by progressive degeneration of the cerebellum and its connections, along with spinal cord involvement. Symptoms typically include gait and coordination difficulties, speech problems and abnormal eye movements. Depending on the subtype, additional symptoms such as muscle stiffness, tremors and cognitive impairment may occur. SCA is caused by genetic mutations, with over 40 known subtypes identified. While there is no cure, management focuses on symptom relief and supportive therapies, such as physical and occupational therapy, to improve mobility and quality of life for affected individuals.[10]

Although the health conditions described above appear disparate, many share common brain pathophysiologies that cause players in this sports modality to exhibit similar motor limitations. These brain pathophysiologies will be described and presented schematically to facilitate the reader's understanding of the broader picture.

Brain Pathophysiology

Injuries to the developing brain can result from various causes, leading to different clinical symptoms and levels of severity. The three most applied classifications in CP football are: (1) according to the impaired brain area, (2) according to the parts of the body involved (i.e., body topography) and (3) considering the degrees of damage (i.e., gross motor function classification system).

Classification According to the Area Involvement

Football players with brain injury can present with a wide range of clinical manifestations that limit their sporting participation. For a better understanding of these manifestations, the Surveillance for Cerebral Palsy in Europe (SCPE) proposed a classification according to the type of impairment considering four subtype groups: (1) injury to the cerebral cortex or pyramidal pathway, commonly manifested by spasticity; (2) basal ganglia lesion, commonly manifested by dyskinesia (dystonic and choreo/athetosis); (3) cerebellar injury, manifesting as ataxia.[11] This classification is also considered by the International Classification of Cerebral Palsy Football (IFCPF) (see Figure 1.1).[12]

Cerebral Cortex Area Involved (Pyramidal Pathway Lesions)

Spastic Hypertonia. Spasticity is often a clinical manifestation that occurs when the neural circuits leading from the cortex to the spinal cord (pyramidal pathway) are damaged. This form of hypertonia is characterised by increased muscle tone, where resistance to passive movement increases with the velocity

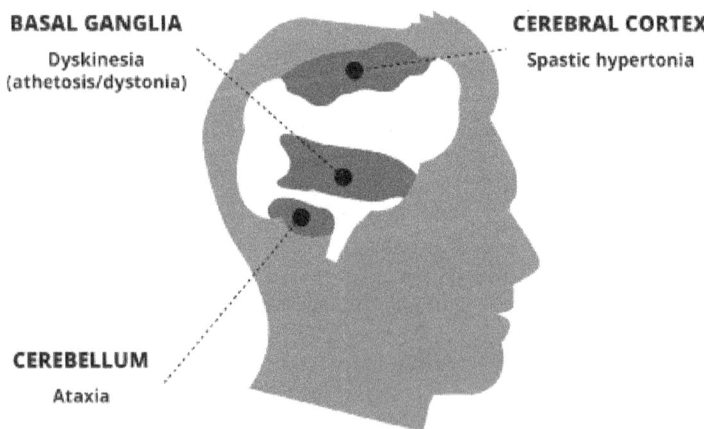

Figure 1.1 Classification of brain injury by area of involvement.

of motion, often presenting as a spastic catch. This resistance can fluctuate depending on the movement's direction.[13] To be recognised as spasticity, a condition must exhibit at least one of the following features: (1) increased resistance to externally applied movement, intensifying with the speed of stretching, or (2) resistance to externally imposed movement that swiftly surpasses a designated speed or joint angle threshold.[14] This component frequently accompanies hyperreflexia, clonus and a positive Babinski sign.[13] This impairment can impact both voluntary motor skills and involuntary muscle contraction. Moreover, spasticity in younger individuals often coexists with progressive musculoskeletal conditions throughout childhood and into later life.[15] As growth progresses, lower-limb issues often arise due to imbalances in the structure of the muscle-tendon unit, resulting in contractures, excessive stretching of muscles and twists in developing bones. Additionally, joint problems such as subluxation and dislocation may develop, especially in the hips and ankles.[15]

The main limitations shown by athletes are associated with difficulties in coordination, particularly between agonist/antagonist muscles, which affects jumping skills, acceleration or deceleration and changing direction during football performance.[16]

Basal Ganglia Area Involved (Extrapyramidal Lesions)

Dyskinesia (Athetosis/Dystonia). Dyskinesia is known for being part of the group of hyperkinetic signs, distinguishable from hypertonia by their presentation. Whereas hypertonia is detectable only during passive movement, hyperkinetic movements occur during any action, whether voluntary or involuntary. This group of conditions constitutes a subset of motor irregularities associated with 'extrapyramidal' movement. Therefore, this classification encompasses impairments that exhibit varying degrees and changes of tone. Within this framework, one can observe dystonic movements and choreoathetotic or athetosis movements in individuals with brain injury.

Dystonia. Dystonia presents as an involuntary shift (i.e., fluctuation) in muscle activation patterns during voluntary movement or while maintaining posture. Dystonia is not necessarily a primary disorder of tone, but it may appear as such due to the inability to fully relax the muscles. It is typically recognised through the observation of abnormal, contorted postures or repetitive movements. This condition exhibits sensitivity to voluntary movement, often worsening with attempts at motion and varying in severity over time. The manifestation of dystonic postures can vary depending on factors such as body position, ongoing tasks, emotional state and level of consciousness. During voluntary movement, individuals may experience sustained involuntary muscle contractions, while muscle tone and activity may appear normal or reduced during rest.[14] The impact of the dystonia is not always apparent.

The pattern and intensity of involuntary muscle activity may also fluctuate, influenced by a variety of factors including the level of arousal, emotional state, tactile stimulation or the degree of engagement in a task.

Football players with this condition often experience co-contraction of antagonistic muscle groups, leading to immediate resistance against rapid directional changes. These fluctuations in muscle tone can cause sudden, involuntary movements in isolated or postural muscle groups. Such involuntary movements can limit a player's ability to accelerate, decelerate and change direction effectively. Additionally, when these impairments affect posture and the upper limbs, they can also hinder the arm swing necessary for efficient running.

Athetosis. Athetosis manifests as slow, continuous, involuntary writhing movements, disrupting the ability to maintain a stable posture.[17] Typically affecting the distal extremities such as hands or feet more than the proximal ones, it can also extend to involve the face, neck and trunk.

Distinguishing athetosis from other movement disorders can be nuanced. While it lacks the sustained postures seen in dystonia, it often co-occurs with dystonia, posing challenges in practical differentiation. Compared to the rapid and jerky movements of chorea, athetotic movements generally exhibit a slower and smoother quality, although exceptions exist. Additionally, athetosis contrasts with tremors and stereotypies due to its absence of rhythmicity and repeatability.[17]

Football players with athetosis frequently exhibit continuous, writhing involuntary movements, which can significantly hinder their ability to control the ball, particularly during interactions with opponents. These players often display issues with movement control and precision. Rapid actions necessitate bodily adjustments for stabilisation, complicating control during dynamic challenges. Additionally, heading accuracy may be intermittently involved in athletes with athetosis or chorea. Athetoid players also face difficulties in speech production and may exhibit pronounced, uncontrollable facial movements.

Cerebellum Area Involved (Extrapyramidal Lesions)

Ataxia. Ataxia typically arises from dysfunction in the cerebellum, or compromised input to the cerebellum from the vestibular or proprioceptive systems. Its manifestation can vary: its evolution, however, is not always the same, since in some conditions it is progressive, as in the genetically caused spinocerebellar ataxias, but in others it may occur suddenly, as in the cases of cerebellar stroke, haemorrhage or infections.[18] In adults, the more common causes of acute ataxia are stroke and tumour, but in children, it is associated with CP, although it is not the most common clinical manifestation.

Ataxia can be grouped into different types, but the two more common clinical manifestations are sensory and motor ataxia (cerebellar ataxia). Sensory ataxia is caused by the impairment of the somatosensory nerve, leading to the interruption of sensory feedback signals, which causes coordination problems. On the other hand, cerebellar ataxia is characterised by a loss of body muscle coordination caused by cerebellar impairment.[19] Symptoms and signs of cerebellar lesions may vary depending on the location. Injury on one side of the cerebellum typically manifests with clinical symptoms on the same side of the body, while generalised involvement leads to more symmetrical symptoms. Additionally, injuries to the cerebellar hemisphere tend to cause limb ataxia, whereas lesions of the vermis result in trunk and gait ataxia with relatively unaffected limbs. Vestibulocerebellar impairments commonly manifest as balance issues or disequilibrium, vertigo and gait ataxia.[19] In parasport contexts, the most accepted concept to describe ataxia as a coordination problem is manifested by irregular rhythm and amplitude movements.[20] Only players with motor ataxia, but not sensory ataxia, can participate.

Football players with ataxia typically demonstrate enhanced running speed, yet frequently encounter difficulties in executing precise tasks such as ball reception and delivery, and controlled movements. Despite this, they generally exhibit proficient synchronisation of arm and leg movements, which minimally impacts their performance and enables effective pivoting in both directions. While dynamic balance may surpass static balance in these players, instances of balance impairment necessitate compensatory measures such as lowering the centre of gravity or widening the base of support. Additionally, maintaining proximity of the arms to the body aids in stabilisation, facilitating balance and control during gameplay. Coordination deficits are evident across various phases of football skills execution, including preparation, execution and recovery, particularly in tasks requiring speed and power.

Topography Classification

This classification groups individuals based on the localisation and distribution of neuromotor impairment, particularly in spastic profiles. There are five principal groups, described in Figure 1.2, which are associated with different aetiological factors:[21]

Tetraparesis

Characterised by severe and symmetric involvement of all four limbs and trunk, tetraparesis in individuals with CP suggests severe perinatal asphyxia at term, postnatal infection (such as bacterial meningitis) and genetic or metabolic disorders. This condition is manifested as spasticity and/or dyskinesia impairments.

Diparesis

Represented by the involvement of all four limbs but with greater spasticity and weakness in the lower limbs, diparesis suggests periventricular leukomalacia due to prematurity and low birth weight. This is characteristic of individuals with CP, usually manifesting as spasticity impairments.

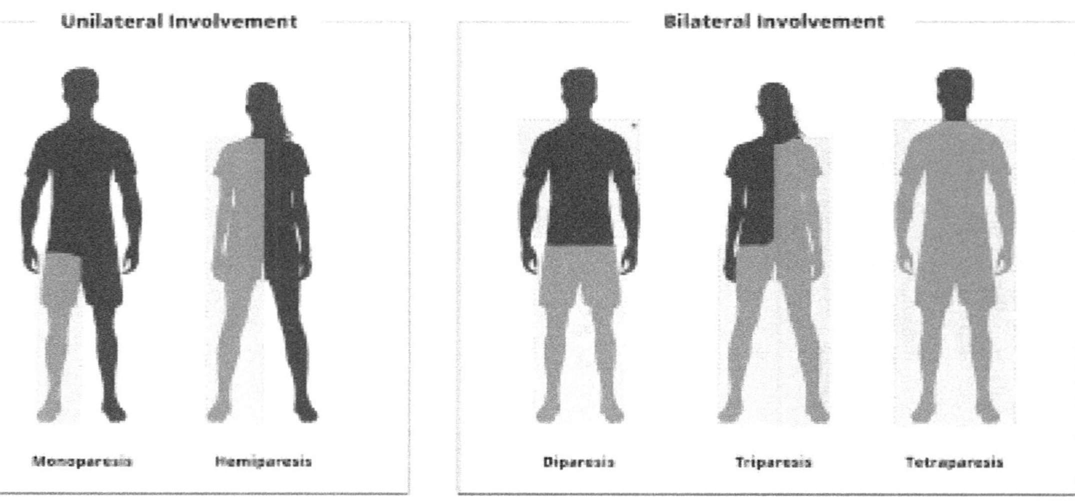

Figure 1.2 Topographical classification according to brain damage. **In some cases, it is possible to observe some impact also in the upper part of the body.*

Hemiparesis

Involving the upper and lower limbs on one side of the body, hemiparesis in individuals with CP suggests perinatal stroke, periventricular haemorrhagic infarction or neonatal cortical infarction. In individuals with stroke, it is characteristic of damage to the middle cerebral or anterior cerebral artery and is the most frequently observed clinical manifestation in this group.[8]

Triparesis

Manifested by the involvement of three limbs, triparesis is usually associated with spasticity or dyskinesia impairments.

Monoparesis

Characterised by the involvement of only one limb, monoparesis is usually manifested as spasticity or dystonia.

While various aetiologies attempt to elucidate the topographical classification, this information lacks complete accuracy and should therefore be approached with caution. In CP football, most participants typically present with spastic hemiplegia, stemming from either CP or acquired brain injury, followed by diplegia and quadriplegia. Ataxia commonly manifests globally across all four limbs. Dyskinesia often presents in a localised form within the limbs (as seen in dystonia), globally across all four limbs (as in athetosis), or in a mixed form alongside spasticity.

Gross Motor Function Classification System (GMFCS)

This classification system, specifically validated for individuals with CP, serves as an international standard, allowing categorisation based on individuals' level of mobility.[22] Professionals utilise this tool to assess current motor function characteristics and determine necessary equipment for daily activities, such as crutches, walking frames or wheelchairs. The classification comprises five levels, with level I representing individuals with fewer limitations, capable of running and walking without major difficulty, while level V includes those with the most severe motor function limitations, requiring assistance for mobility.[6,23] In the context of this discussion, football players typically fall into levels I and II of the GMFCS, indicating independent walking and running abilities. However, instances may arise where a goalkeeper is categorised under GMFCS level III (see Figure 1.3).

Figure 1.3 Graphical representation of the five levels of the GMFCS and highlights those in which football players with CP are grouped (adapted from E&R © Robert Palisano, Peter Rosenbaum, Doreen Bartlett, Michael Livingston, 2007 CanChild Centre for Childhood Disability Research, McMaster University).[22]

Conclusions and Practical Applications

In conclusion, CP football is witnessing a surge in popularity and offers significant opportunities for individuals with various brain pathologies who maintain ambulant profiles to actively participate in sports. This chapter has focused on delineating these profiles, underscoring the importance of recognising the intricate neuronal networks within the nervous system and the unique neural plasticity that enables diverse degrees of adaptation following injury. This adaptability is influenced by physiological and contextual elements, including individual and environmental factors. Consequently, each athlete's response to injury will be unique, leading to distinct manifestations of impairment and activity limitations.

Therefore, it is imperative to stress the necessity of coordinating the information from this chapter with the classification rules outlined for this para-sport, as detailed in Chapter 5 of this book. This coordinated approach ensures that professionals and practitioners can accurately assess individuals and place them in the most suitable categories for participation in cerebral palsy football. Such alignment not only enhances the inclusivity and effectiveness of the sport but also fosters the overall well-being and enjoyment of the participants.

2 Barriers and Facilitators to Improve Physical Activity and Sport in Individuals with CP

Alba Roldan, María Isabel Cornejo and Heather Jameson

Contextual Framework

To promote physical activity, particularly football, among young people with CP and other acquired brain injuries, it is crucial to consider disability as a multidimensional phenomenon arising from the intricate daily interaction between the individual and their environment. This interaction is effectively elucidated by the ICF, which serves as a conceptual framework facilitating the use of common language in describing disability and its associated factors. The ICF framework helps delineate the components of health and well-being and explicates the outcomes of the interaction between functioning and disability (see Figure 2.1).

The ICF framework is divided into two main parts: 'Functioning and Disability' and 'Contextual Factors'. Here is a brief description of each part:

Functioning and Disability

Body Functions and Structures

This domain pertains to changes that may occur in bodily functions (e.g., physiological functioning of body systems, including psychological functions) and changes in structures (e.g., anatomical parts such as organs, limbs and their components). For example, CP could be classified within the ICF framework as (1) an impairment in brain structure [body structure impairment] and (2) resulting in a functional impairment of voluntary movement control [body function impairment].

Activities

This domain encompasses essential areas such as tasks and actions of daily living. It evaluates the individual's ability to perform these tasks in their

DOI: 10.4324/9781032708942-2

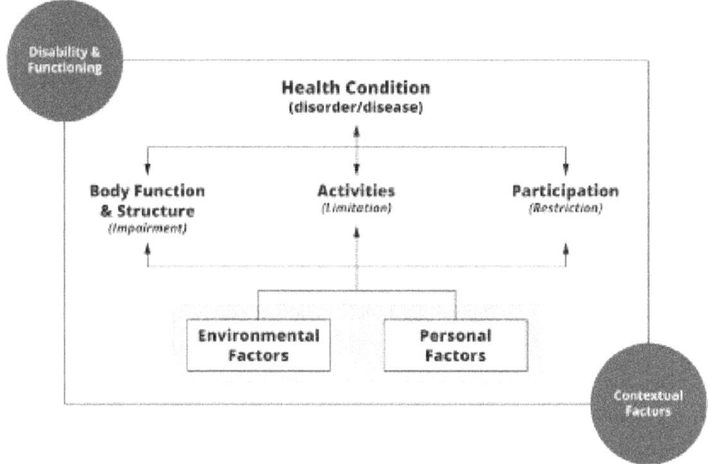

Figure 2.1 Graphical representation of the ICF (adapted from the WHO, 2001).[24]

actual environment. For instance, in an individual with CP, the assessment would focus on their ability to walk or run.

Participation

This domain reflects the outcome of the interaction between the aforementioned two domains. Depending on functional and/or structural impairment, a person may or may not be able to engage in certain activities. This capability, or lack thereof, impacts their participation in their environment. For example, an individual with CP who cannot walk would not be able to participate in CP football, which is played by ambulant profiles. They would need to seek an alternative activity in which to engage.

Contextual Factors

These factors influence functioning in specific life situations and are divided into two categories.

Environmental Factors (External)

These refer to all external elements (e.g., natural and social environment) that decisively impact a person's functioning. Examples include architectural structures, social policies, transportation networks, materials, opportunities, etc.

Personal Factors (Internal)

These refer to innate characteristics of the individual that are not part of their health condition, as well as aspects related to their life situation. These factors may include gender, race, age, other associated comorbidities, physical status, lifestyle, living habits, upbringing, coping styles, social background, education, profession, past and current experiences (life events), general behaviour patterns, character style, individual psychological assets and other personal traits.

It is important to note that contextual factors can function as barriers or facilitators depending on characteristics of the physical, social and/or attitudinal world.[24] In the next section, we will delve deeper into the factors that seem to most significantly hinder the promotion and adherence of individuals with cerebral palsy to sports practice.

Barriers and Other Considerations to the Practice of Football among Individuals with CP

Individuals with CP often view physical activity as a crucial means to discover their identity and find their place within the community. Engaging in physical activity not only helps them connect socially, allowing them to bond with friends and meet new people, but also offers a sense of freedom from the limitations imposed by their disability. Despite these significant benefits, research indicates that individuals with CP participate in physical activity at much lower levels compared to their peers without disabilities, due to various barriers.[25] These barriers include personal factors such as pain, fatigue, and motor impairments, as well as environmental factors like lack of accessible facilities and social support. Physical activity is crucial for individuals with CP as it enhances overall health, improving cardiorespiratory fitness, muscle strength and motor function, while also contributing to better mental health and social integration. Encouraging regular physical activity can significantly mitigate the risks of secondary health complications, such as cardiovascular diseases and obesity, thereby improving the quality of life for individuals with CP.[26] Since the barriers are multifaceted and the group with CP is very heterogeneous, in this section we will focus on those barriers that can have the most negative impact when promoting the practice of CP Football in this population according to the different stages of life.

Childhood

Age-related barriers to physical activity for children with CP are substantial and complex. A primary obstacle is the absence of customised programmes and opportunities that meet the specific needs of these children. Research indicates that many existing physical activity initiatives fail to adequately address the diverse requirements of children with CP, limiting their participation. A critical contributing factor is the inadequate training of professionals responsible for providing physical activity, including physical therapists, healthcare providers and educational and sport professionals. These individuals often lack the expertise needed to accurately assess and recommend activities that are both appropriate and engaging for individuals with CP. This shortfall in professional knowledge can severely limit access to suitable PA options, further hindering the involvement of children with CP in physical activities.

Another significant barrier is the limited availability of practice opportunities specifically tailored to the needs of children with CP. Even when such opportunities exist, they are often scarce, and parents may be unaware of them. This lack of awareness can prevent children from accessing valuable physical activity resources that could enhance their physical and mental well-being. In this context, the role of healthcare and educational professionals becomes crucial. Their involvement can be pivotal in disseminating information about available physical activity opportunities and encouraging participation. Developing life skills in children with CP is also essential for their effective engagement in physical activity in adulthood.

Similarly, the lack of training among sports coaches in designing physical activity programmes for children with CP is a significant issue. These children require tailored programmes that address their unique needs, yet many professionals lack the necessary expertise. Without proper training, coaches may inadvertently design activities that are ineffective or even harmful. By equipping coaches and teachers with the right skills and knowledge, we can ensure that children with CP receive the full benefits of physical activity, tailored to their specific needs.[27] This approach will help promote and recruit more children who can practise CP football. For example, a child with CP with walking ability, if they do not use any assistive devices and walk without any problems, would benefit from an inclusive practice environment with other children of the same age, where significant adaptations are not necessary. Alternatively, a specific football club for children with CP could be suitable. If the impact of CP is more significant but the child can still walk without support, the ideal would be to look for a CP football club. Lastly, if the child requires assistive devices such as crutches, walkers or even a wheelchair for longer distances, finding a Frame Football club would be ideal (see Figure 2.2).

Lack of time is another significant barrier to physical activity for children with CP, impacting their overall health and development. Most children with CP are required to follow extensive and demanding therapies necessary to manage their condition and improve their quality of life. The more severe the disability, the more numerous and intense these therapies are, making play and therapy mutually exclusive activities. Moreover, participation in these therapies and other medical appointments leads to physical exhaustion, increasing chronic fatigue in children with CP and promoting sedentary behaviours. This situation often leads to late engagement in physical activity, normally after

Figure 2.2 Different alternatives for practicing football for individuals with CP.

the age of 18, when most therapeutic treatments are over. This delayed participation results in prolonged inactivity and fewer health benefits. Moreover, this delayed participation often results in a downward spiral of physical and functional decline, underscoring the necessity of early and sustained physical activity interventions (see Figure 2.3).

Combining therapeutic exercise with leisure physical activities is essential for children with CP to cultivate healthy and active behaviours from an early age. Regular involvement in both types of activities improves physical functioning, social participation and overall quality of life.[28] Considering physical activities, such as playing football, as complementary to therapies is important. This integrated approach aims to achieve interdisciplinary common goals, fostering positive adherence to sport and physical exercise, and avoiding decreased interest in physical activity with age.

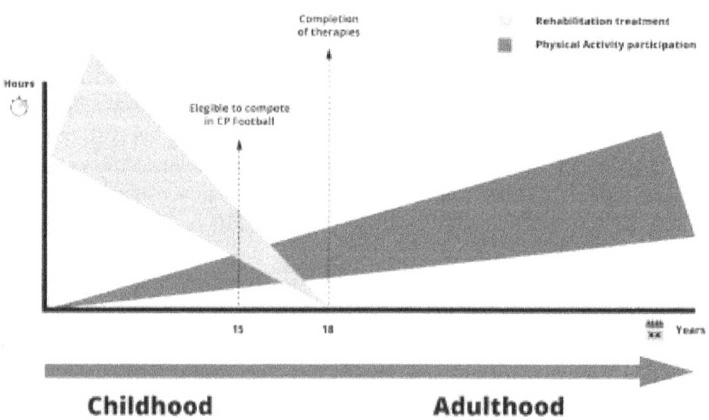

Figure 2.3 Therapy treatments and physical activity participation display along lifespan in children with CP.

Adolescence and Early Adulthood

Physical activity is also crucial for maintaining health and well-being in adolescents and adults with CP. However, they face significant barriers that hinder their participation in regular exercise. Many of the barriers identified in childhood continue to appear in these stages, such as the lack of training of sports specialists to respond to this group. However, in this section, we will focus on the lack of information on guidelines for exercise testing and prescription in young people and adults with CP and how this information is closely related to the severity of the disability. The authors of this chapter consider this information to be important because it is at this age that initiation into sport performance, in our case, initiation into competitive football, is likely to begin.

The American College of Sports Medicine (ACSM) is regarded as a reference resource for exercise management in individuals with chronic diseases and disabilities. Their comprehensive guidelines provide evidence-based recommendations to optimise health, enhance functional capacity and improve the quality of life for this population, ensuring safe and effective exercise practices. However, these recommendations are scarce when it comes to individuals with CP. Although useful, they have significant limitations, especially as the severity of the individual's condition increases. The general guidelines of the ACSM do not specifically address the particular needs of people with different levels of CP severity, leading to a lack of clarity and applicability in many cases.

Additionally, the available literature is predominantly focused on children and adolescents, as CP is a congenital disability. This focus on younger individuals leaves a significant gap in knowledge and resources available for adults with CP. The existing research does not adequately address the needs and challenges faced by adults, hindering the development of appropriate physical exercise programmes or assessment tools for this population.[29] For example, the GMFCS, widely used to assess motor function in individuals with CP, is validated only up to 18 years of age, limiting its applicability in the evaluation of adults.[30] This lack of information and resources makes it difficult to promote and evaluate athletic performance in adults with CP. Without adequate tools and studies, it is complicated to plan training sessions that meet individual needs, the specific requirements of the sport and performance goals. The absence of clear and validated guidelines for adults with CP creates challenges for both healthcare professionals and sports coaches, who must adapt general recommendations based on a limited understanding of the specific needs of adults with CP.[31]

In the case of CP football, recent studies have placed significant emphasis on the validation and reliability of various assessment tests, which are crucial for evaluating the functional abilities and performance levels of CP football players, providing a foundation for effective training and classification.

Although these topics will be addressed later in various chapters related to the physical assessment of athletes, some of these tests include linear sprints or the change-of-direction ability, among others. These tests allow differentiation between different classes of CP football players, highlighting their utility in classification processes. In the performance orientation, various football-specific tests that require ball dribbling, such as the Stop and Go test and Turning and Dribbling tests, have been validated for the CP population, having the ability to discriminate among classes and being resistant to training and competitive levels.[32]

The classification in para sports determines who can or cannot compete, considering the 'eligible impairment' and its impact on 'activity limitation' during sport practice. A lack of information about the classification in para sports can create significant barriers, leading to unrealistic expectations regarding participation in certain disciplines. For this reason, this book will address this issue in Chapter 5 of this book. In summary, the work being undertaken in the field of CP football, with the validation of various functional tests tailored to a specific sport and demographic, is proving capable of differentiating between different levels of functionality in adults. These studies are helping to build a body of knowledge that can significantly aid the promotion of physical and sporting activities for young people and adults with CP. Additionally, this book is improving the resources and information available to enhance the training of sports coaches.

Conclusions and Practical Applications

Barriers to physical activity often exhibit a dichotomous nature; once effectively addressed, they transform into facilitators, underscoring their dual potential. For example, time constraints, commonly cited as a barrier, can be reinterpreted and resolved by integrating exercise into therapy and educational daily routines, thereby turning an obstacle into an opportunity. Similarly, lack of motivation can be countered by creating engaging, goal-oriented fitness programmes and adapting activities appropriately to individuals with CP.

In the realm of CP football, recognising and prioritising the most significant barriers is essential for effective promotion and participation. These barriers can vary significantly based on age, severity of disability and contextual factors. Younger participants may face issues such as accessibility (i.e., practical opportunities), lack of awareness about functional potential, or parental support, while older individuals might grapple with physical limitations or motivational challenges. The severity of disability also dictates specific needs; those with more profound impairments may require specialised equipment, tailored training programmes or personalised coaching strategies to ensure they can participate fully and safely.

Identifying and addressing these barriers is not merely about overcoming hurdles but about transforming them into stepping stones that facilitate engagement and participation. This approach ensures that individuals of all ages and abilities can enjoy the benefits of physical activity, particularly in sports like CP football, where tailored support can significantly enhance the experience and outcomes for participants. By converting barriers into facilitators, we can create a more inclusive and empowering landscape for physical activity and CP football.

3 The History of CP Football

Sam Turner, Tom Langen and Raúl Reina

Contextual Framework

Origins of CP Football and Development

CP football, known as 7-a-side football within the Paralympic Games, has been developing since the early 1970s through physical activities in schools for individuals with disabilities, at a time when awareness and understanding of disabilities were gaining momentum.[33] The concept of CP football emerged to adapt the traditional 11-a-side football format for individuals with CP, enabling them to participate fully and competitively in the game. The 7-a-side format, with smaller teams and adapted rules, was structured to provide a more inclusive and balanced platform for athletes with CP, allowing them to showcase their skills and compete in a way that suited their abilities. The evolution of the rules and gameplay in CP football has been a dynamic process and, initially, the Para sport adopted many elements from mainstream football but made essential modifications to accommodate the needs of athletes with CP.

One of the primary challenges faced by CP football athletes is the physical limitation imposed by their condition. CP affects muscle tone, movement and coordination, which can make playing football particularly demanding. Athletes must undergo rigorous and often painful physical therapy to improve their mobility and strength. Despite these efforts, they may still experience muscle spasticity, balance issues and fatigue that can affect their performance on the field.[33] For instance, CP football is played on a smaller field, with seven players on each team instead of the usual 11.[34] Its development pursued to ensure that the sport remained accessible and enjoyable for individuals with disabilities, especially for ambulant para-athletes with CP and related brain injuries. The Para sport not only allows individuals with CP to engage in competitive physical activity but also promotes social integration, boosts self-esteem and enhances overall quality of life.[35]

A pivotal moment in the history of CP football was the formation of the Cerebral Palsy International Sports and Recreation Association (CPISRA) in 1978. CPISRA played a crucial role in promoting and organising sports for

DOI: 10.4324/9781032708942-3

individuals with CP, including football. The establishment of CPISRA marked the beginning of a structured approach to developing and governing CP sports on an international level. As an international sport, it was first played in 1978 at the third International Cerebral Palsy Games held in Edinburgh (Scotland), organised by CPISRA. In the subsequent decades, CP football saw significant milestones that contributed to its growth and recognition. The first official international CP football tournament was held in 1982 in Greve (Denmark), paving the way for more structured competitions and international participation. This tournament brought together players from various countries with Ireland reining victorious, while also highlighting the need for global recognition of CP football. In this timeline, the first regional championships were held in Glasgow (Scotland), in 1985. As the sport gained momentum, efforts were directed towards formalising the rules and regulations specific to CP football. The inclusion of various classifications, based on the severity of the cerebral palsy, allowed for a level playing field, ensuring fair competition for athletes with different abilities.

A significant milestone occurred in October 2010 when the general assembly of CPISRA adopted a motion for CP football to become an independent Para sport. In January 2015, the IFCPF became the governing body of the Para sport. Both CPISRA and IFCPF worked alongside for five years, and, in 2014, a new format of football, Frame Football, was developed for players requiring the use of posture control walkers/frames.

In terms of talent development, 2015 saw the inaugural IFCPF CP Football World Championships U19, taking place at the CPISRA World Games in Nottingham (England), with seven teams from three regions. Other U19 competitions were also held in São Paulo (Brazil) at the 2017 Youth Parapan American Games (six countries), the 2017 European ParaYouth Games in Genoa (Italy) with three teams and the 2018 CPISRA World Games in Sant Cugat (Spain) with the participation of three teams from three different regions.

Another strategic development aspect was Female CP football. For the vast majority of CP football history, the focus has been almost exclusively on the men's game, following the trend of mainstream football. While other Para sports have focused on utilising mixed-gender participation as a way to create sports opportunities (e.g., Boccia or wheelchair rugby), the IFCPF has taken the time to speak to female players and non-players to get their feedback and insight for the game they want to play. In January 2017, IFCPF Tournament Regulations were amended to stimulate tournaments to be played mixed gender, other than in Regional and World Level competitions. This rule to allow mixed gender teams was a development tool intended to grow female participation until the numbers become sufficient to have female-specific teams and competitions, having the first female-specific international-level competition in 2022.

The current state of CP football reflects a blend of progress and ongoing challenges. On the one hand, the sport has made significant strides in terms of visibility, participation (with specific actions for those with more severe impairments, younger players and women), and competitive standards. On the other hand, the removal from the Paralympic Games programme after Rio 2016 significantly impacted national programmes' development and funding.

CP Football in the Paralympic Games

The inclusion of CP football in the Paralympic Games underscores the sport's significant development and the commitment of its supporters. CP football made its inaugural appearance at the Paralympic Games in New York in 1984 and continued to be a mainstay of the Paralympic programme until the 2016 Rio Games.[36] This inclusion represented not only a milestone for the sport but also a substantial advancement in the wider movement for disability sports.

The integration of CP football into the Paralympic Games provided a prestigious global platform for para-athletes with CP to demonstrate their skills and compete at the highest level. The prominence and prestige of the Paralympics attracted increased media attention, sponsorship and funding, which facilitated the growth of the sport at both grassroots and elite levels.[37] This support allowed the Para sport to be incorporated into national mainstream structures, such as those in England, the Netherlands and the USA. The visibility of CP football in the Paralympics inspired many young individuals with CP to participate in the sport, as they saw athletes with similar conditions competing on an international stage. This visibility served as a powerful motivator, helping to dismantle stereotypes and misconceptions about disability. Furthermore, it fostered a sense of pride and accomplishment among athletes, contributing significantly to their personal development and social integration.[38]

Athletes with CP first competed in the Paralympic Games in Arnhem in 1980, but CP football was officially included in the Paralympic programme at the New York and Stoke Mandeville Games in 1984. Belgium won the inaugural Paralympic gold medal in CP football, defeating Ireland in the final. The 1984 Games were notable for featuring two separate CP football competitions: one in Stoke Mandeville for wheelchair users and another in New York for ambulant players. CP football continued to feature in every Paralympic Games thereafter (in the ambulant format only) up to the Rio 2016 Games. Between 1988 and 1996, the Netherlands were particularly dominant, securing gold medals in Seoul 1988, Barcelona 1992 and Atlanta 1996. Since the early 2000s, the Paralympic medals have been shared among four nations: Ukraine, Russia, Brazil and Iran (see Table 3.1).

Currently, CP football is not part of the Paralympic programme due to a decision by the International Paralympic Committee (IPC). Following a review of the IFCPF bid for the Tokyo 2020 Paralympic Games, the IPC concluded that the sport did not meet the minimum requirements for global reach. According to former IPC President Sir Philip Craven,

Table 3.1 Synthesis of CP football results at the summer Paralympic Games.

Year	*Host*	*Gold*	*Silver*	*Bronze*	*Teams*
1984	New York (USA)	Belgium	Ireland	Great Britain	6
1988	Seoul (South Korea)	The Netherlands	Belgium	Ireland	5
1992	Barcelona (Spain)	The Netherlands	Portugal	Ireland	8
1996	Atlanta (USA)	The Netherlands	Russia	Spain	8
2000	Sydney (Australia)	Russia	Ukraine	Brazil	8
2004	Athens (Greece)	Ukraine	Brazil	Russia	8
2008	Beijing (China)	Ukraine	Russia	Iran	8
2012	London (United Kingdom)	Russia	Ukraine	Iran	8
2016	Rio de Janeiro (Brazil)	Ukraine	Iran	Brazil	8

> the Board's final decision was not an easy one and, after much debate, we decided not to include two sports – football 7-a-side and sailing – from the Tokyo 2020 programme for the same reason. Both did not fulfil the IPC Handbook's minimum criteria for worldwide reach.[39]

The IPC Handbook stipulates that team sports must be widely and regularly practised in a minimum of 24 countries across three IPC regions, and individual sports in at least 32 countries across three IPC regions, to be considered for inclusion in the Paralympic Games. Despite the IFCPF's demonstration that 29 countries from five regions are affiliated, with a total of 4,210 athletes, the IPC maintained that the global reach criterion had not been met.

CP Football Programmes and Competition Structure

CP football has achieved substantial global recognition, with numerous international tournaments, leagues and programmes dedicated to the development of the Para sport and the para-athletes involved. Nonetheless, further progress is necessary, with ongoing efforts to integrate CP football into mainstream sports culture and expand opportunities for athletes with CP. As of 2024, CP football is practised in 90 countries across all five IPC regions (Table 3.2).

However, access to CP football remains uneven across different regions, with some countries having well-developed programmes and others lacking basic infrastructure and support. Addressing these disparities is crucial for the inclusive growth of the Para sport, with the following international-level competition opportunities sanctioned by IFCPF:

Table 3.2 Countries with CP football programmes.

	AFRICA (13)	*AMERICAS (18)*	*ASIA (27)*	*EUROPE (30)*	*OCEANIA (2)*
WORLD (21)	–	Argentina Brazil Canada Chile Colombia United States Venezuela	Iran Japan South Korea Thailand	England Germany Ireland Italy The Netherlands North Ireland Scotland Spain Ukraine	Australia
REGIONAL (1)	–	Ecuador	–	–	–
INTERNATIONAL DEVELOPMENT (16)	Ghana Nigeria	Panama Peru	Cambodia India Malaysia Myanmar Philippines Singapore	Austria Belgium Denmark Finland Georgia Kazakhstan	–
NATIONAL (3)	South Africa Tunisia	–	Saudi Arabia	–	–

(*Continued*)

Table 3.2 (Continued)

	AFRICA (13)	*AMERICAS (18)*	*ASIA (27)*	*EUROPE (30)*	*OCEANIA (2)*
PARTICIPATION (49)	Algeria	Costa Rica	Bangladesh	Belarus	New Zealand
	Cameroon	Cuba	Brunei	Bosnia and Herzegovina	
	Cape Verde	El Salvador	China	France	
	Congo	Honduras	East Timor	Hungary	
	Egypt	Mexico	Jordan	Luxemburg	
	Kenya	Nicaragua	Kuwait	Malta	
	Sierra Leone	Trinidad and Tobago	Kyrgyzstan	Norway	
	Somalia	Uruguay	Macau	Poland	
	Uganda		Mongolia	Portugal	
			Nepal	Russia*	
			Pakistan	Slovakia	
			Qatar	Sweden	
			Sri Lanka	Switzerland	
			United Arab Emirates	Turkey	
			Vietnam	Wales	

* Included in this category due to the international sanction imposed for doping reasons.

World-Level Competition

World-level competitions represent the highest level of competition in CP football and have been known by various names throughout the sport's history, including World Games, World Championships, Intercontinental Cup and World Cup. Currently, IFCPF hosts two premier tournaments every two years:

IFCPF World Cup

The most prestigious event in the CP football international competition cycle, where the top teams in the world compete to become world champions, for both male and female teams.

IFCPF World Championships

Provides a top-level competition for teams that did not qualify for the World Cup.

Together, these two events form the pinnacle of CP football competition for national teams. The rankings from these tournaments are combined, with teams from the World Cup and World Championships listed together to award ranking points. In 2022, for the first time, 23 teams competed at the highest level of CP football, receiving ranking points accordingly. Table 3.3 summarises the history of CP football activities at this competition level.

Regional-Level Competition

The five aforementioned regions (i.e., Africa, Americas, Asia, Europe and Oceania) are grouped into three for regional development: Africa and the Americas (America Cup), Europe (European Championships) and the Asia-Oceania Championships. This regional grouping presents a significant challenge for the development and sustainability of the Para sport. For instance, only an attempt at the Africa Championships was held in 2018, with only South Africa participating; similarly, Australia stands alone in Oceania. Additionally, there are significant resource disparities among countries in North, Central and South America. Notably, the Parapan American Games are currently the only multi-sport event under the Americas Paralympic Committee where CP football is included in the official programme. Table 3.4 summarises the main activities at the regional level.

Table 3.3 CP football history at world-level competition.

Year	*Title*	*Host*	*Gold*	*Silver*	*Bronze*	*Teams*
1978	International Cerebral Palsy Games	Edinburgh (Scotland)	*No Data*	*No Data*	*No Data*	*No Data*
1982	CPISRA International Cerebral Palsy Games	Greve (Denmark)	Ireland	The Netherlands	*No Data*	*No Data*
1986	CPISRA International Cerebral Palsy Games	Gits (Belgium)	The Netherlands	Belgium	*No Data*	6
1990	CPISRA World Championships	Assen (The Netherlands)	The Netherlands	Ireland	Belgium	5
1994	CPISRA World Championships	Dublin (Ireland)	The Netherlands	Ireland	Belgium	5
1998	CPISRA World Championships	Rio de Janeiro (Brazil)	Russia	Ukraine	Brazil	11
2001	CPISRA World Games	Nottingham (England)	Ukraine	Russia	Brazil	13
2003	CPISRA World Championships	Buenos Aires (Argentina)	Ukraine	Brazil	Russia	12
2005	CPISRA World Championships	New London (USA)	Russia	Ukraine	Iran	13
2007	CPISRA World Championships	Rio de Janeiro (Brazil)	Russia	Iran	Ukraine	16
2009	CPISRA International Championships	Arnhem (The Netherlands)	Ukraine	Russia	Iran	11
2011	CPISRA World Championships	Assen (The Netherlands)	Russia	Iran	Ukraine	16
2013	CPISRA Intercontinental Cup	Sant Cugat (Spain)	Ukraine	Brazil	Russia	16
2015	IFCPF World Championships	Burton-upon-Trent (England)	Russia	Ukraine	Brazil	15
2017	IFCPF World Championships	San Luis (Argentina)	Ukraine	Iran	Russia	16
2019	IFCPF World Cup	Seville (Spain)	Russia	Ukraine	Brazil	16
2022	IFCPF Men's World Cup	Salou (Spain)	Ukraine	Iran	Brazil	15
2022	IFCPF Women's World Cup	Salou (Spain)	USA	Australia	Japan	5
2022	IFCPF Men's World Championships	Olbia, Italy	Colombia	Scotland	Japan	8

Table 3.4 CP football history at regional-level competition.

Year	*Title*	*Host*	*Gold*	*Silver*	*Bronze*	*Teams*
1985	*No Data*	Glasgow (Scotland)	*No Data*	*No Data*	*No Data*	*No Data*
1989	Robin Hood Games	Nottingham (England)	The Netherlands	Ireland	*No Data*	*No Data*
1991	CPISRA European Championships	Nottingham (England)	The Netherlands	England	*No Data*	*No Data*
1995	CPISRA European Championships	Nottingham (England)	The Netherlands	Russia	*No Data*	*No Data*
1995	CPISRA Americas Championships	Buenos Aires (Argentina)	*No Data*	*No Data*	*No Data*	*No Data*
1999	CPISRA European Championships	Brasschaat (Belgium)	Ukraine	The Netherlands	*No Data*	*No Data*
1999	CPISRA Americas Championships	Buenos Aires (Argentina)	Argentina	USA	Brazil	4
2002	CPISRA European Championships	Kiev (Ukraine)	Ukraine	Russia	The Netherlands	7
2002	CPIRSA Asia Championships	Busan (South Korea)	*No Data*	*No Data*	*No Data*	*No Data*
2002	CPISRA Americas Championships	Santiago (Chile)	Brazil	Argentina	USA	4
2006	CPISRA European Championships	Dublin (Ireland)	Ukraine	Russia	The Netherlands	8
2006	CPIRSA Asia Championships	Kuala Lumpur (Malaysia)	Iran	Australia	China	6
2007	CPISRA Americas Championships	Rio de Janeiro (Brazil)	Brazil	Argentina	Canada	6
2010	CPISRA European Championships	Glasgow (Scotland)	Ukraine	Russia	Ireland	10
2010	CPISRA Americas Championships	Buenos Aires (Argentina)	Brazil	USA	Argentina	6
2010	Asian Para Games	Guangzhou (China)	Iran	China	Japan	4
2014	CPISRA European Championships	Maia (Portugal)	Ukraine	The Netherlands	Russia	11
2014	Asian Para Games	Incheon (South Korea)	Iran	Japan	South Korea	4
2015	Para PanAmerican Games	Toronto (Canada)	Brazil	Argentina	USA	6
2018	IFCPF European Championships	Zeist (The Netherlands)	Russia	Ukraine	Ireland	10
2018	IFCPF Americas Championships	Quito (Ecuador)	Brazil	Argentina	USA	8
2018	IFCPF Asia-Oceania Championships	Kish Island (Iran)	Iran	Australia	Jordan	5
2023	IFCPF European Championships	Oristano (Italy)	Ukraine	England	Spain	8
2023	IFCPF Men's Asia-Oceania Championships	Melbourne (Australia)	Iran	Australia	Thailand	5
2023	IFCPF Women's Asia-Oceania Championships	Melbourne (Australia)	Australia	Japan	Nepal	3
2023	Para PanAmerican Games	Santiago (Chile)	Brazil	Argentina	USA	6

Club World Cup

To strengthen the club football programmes that underpin international competition programmes, IFCPF also hosts an international competition for club teams. The inaugural competition was held in 2022 in Barcelona, Spain, with the participation of seven teams from Denmark, England, Ireland, Japan, the Netherlands, Spain and the USA.

Conclusions and Practical Applications

CP football has undergone significant development since its inception in the early 1970s, evolving into a globally recognised Para sport with international tournaments, leagues and developmental programmes. This growth was underscored by its inclusion in the Paralympic Games from 1984 to 2016, which provided a prestigious platform, increased visibility and attracted media attention, sponsorship and funding. Despite its removal from the Paralympic programme post-Rio 2016, CP football continues to thrive, practised in 90 countries across all five IPC regions as of 2024. However, access to CP football remains uneven, with some regions lacking the necessary support and infrastructure. To address these disparities, the IFCPF organises premier tournaments such as the IFCPF World Cup and World Championships, as well as regional competitions like the America Cup, European Championships and Asia-Oceania Championships, fostering local talent and providing competitive opportunities. The Club World Cup, introduced in 2022, further strengthens club-level football. Ensuring equitable access across regions involves building infrastructure, training coaches and officials and securing funding. Expanding programmes for younger athletes, women and those with severe impairments, alongside initiatives like Frame Football and mixed-gender teams, promotes inclusivity. CP football significantly enhances social integration, self-esteem and quality of life for athletes with CP, helping to break down stereotypes about disabilities. Continued efforts to highlight athletes' achievements and stories will inspire future generations and promote greater acceptance and support for individuals with disabilities in sports. While CP football has achieved remarkable growth, ongoing efforts are needed to address regional disparities, enhance infrastructure and integrate the sport into mainstream culture, providing valuable opportunities for athletes with CP and fostering competitive excellence and social inclusion.

4 The Rules of CP Football and Development of CP Football Officials

Skye Arthur-Banning and Margaret Domka

Contextual Framework

An essential element in understanding CP football globally, its operation and its place within the disability football landscape is to comprehend the International Football Association Board (IFAB) Laws of the Game and the modifications under which CP football is played. Beyond understanding the game's rules, it is crucial for the growth and development of CP football to know how one can become a CP football referee and the steps necessary to advance as an official. This chapter aims to outline both the rules and the process of becoming a CP football official.

With association football being viewed as the 'Game for the World' with an estimated 250 million participants annually, and billions more fans of international competitions,[40] one might assume that everyone who wishes to play is already playing. Yet, football continues to grow in various populations around the globe, becoming even more inclusive and accommodating. The Fédération Internationale de Football Association (FIFA) released its global women's football landscape survey report in 2023, suggesting that the number of women and girls playing football worldwide increased to an estimated 16,600,000, up by nearly a quarter compared to 2019.[41] While the growth in women's and girls' participation is commendable, there is limited information on how other populations engage with football. Specifically, there is a paucity of information about the rates at which people with disabilities participate and a lack of widespread awareness of the modified rules that enable their participation.

IFAB is the 'independent guardian of the Laws of the Game'[42] and is responsible for setting and making annual changes to the rules of football, commonly known as the 'Laws of the Game'. There are 17 Laws that encompass everything from The Field of Play (Law 1) to Determining the Outcome of a Match (Law 10) and The Penalty Kick (Law 14).[43] Each Law explains in detail how an element of the game is to be carried out, providing insight to referees, coaches, players and fans into how the game is to be played. While updates are made based on new or emerging technologies, tactics and the

DOI: 10.4324/9781032708942-4

protection of players' safety and welfare, the changes are designed to be applied universally. Apart from modifications permitted by IFAB, the Laws must not be modified or changed.[44] It is within this specific exception – 'apart from modifications permitted' – that CP football operates to best serve the players.

In addition, IFAB designates that 'for youth, veterans, disability and grassroots football'[44] certain changes are permitted to make the game suitable for the respective populations. Such opportunities for modification include the size of the field of play, the size and weight of the ball, the duration of halves, the use of substitutes and temporary dismissals. The IFCPF, as an independent International Federation, has chosen to extend some of these changes to best accommodate its playing audience and the various disabilities.

For people with disabilities to fully partake in the 'Beautiful Game', there must be an understanding of how various disabilities may affect the way participants engage with the game. Certainly, upper body limb impairments have less impact than lower body impairments, and neurological disorders have varying degrees of impact. Therefore, Laws should be modified to best accommodate different types of disabilities without altering the nature of the game itself too drastically. CP football is an example of a sport making participation possible for people with certain types of disabilities, allowing them to play football with sensible modifications to the Laws of the Game. These modifications provide increased opportunities for athlete success while ensuring safety and the overall development of the sport.

IFCPF governs all elements of CP football, including the rules, and uses the main IFAB Laws with its own 'IFCPF Modifications to the IFAB Laws of the Game', which outline adjustments to particular Laws to best accommodate the players and their specific disabilities, enhancing success, enjoyment and safety.[45]

The Process of Determining IFCPF Modifications to the Laws of the Game

The process of determining which Laws should have modifications within the IFCPF game is multi-staged and conducted annually so that modifications can be implemented on January 1 of each new competition cycle. The initiation of modifications to the Laws can come from various stakeholders, such as a group of coaches suggesting changes to IFCPF, IFCPF leadership noticing patterns of deficiencies in existing rules during a series of games or the Head of Officials and/or members of the referee committee identifying shortcomings in the Laws that jeopardise fair play and/or player safety. In each situation, it is vital to keep the game entertaining while replicating the IFAB game as closely as possible for fan and player understanding and ultimately to allow athletes to showcase their talent while minimising the risk of injury or harm.

From the initial stakeholder recommendation, the suggested change is drafted, debated and discussed within the referee committee. This committee comprises current or retired referees representing each of the IFCPF participating regions, as well as the Manager of Officials and the Officiating Education Coordinator. This stage is considered the proposal phase of the suggested modification. Specific changes are formally recommended by the Officiating Committee and sent to the Technical Committee. The Technical Committee, also made up of regional representatives along with the Technical Director, Technical Manager, Classification Manager, Officiating Manager and an Athlete Representative, debates and decides whether and how the potential rule change should move forward. Upon a vote of approval, the final rule change recommendation is sent to the IFCPF Management Team for its final modification and approval. If the IFCPF Management Team approves, the modification to the Laws is adopted in the next full-year cycle of rule changes put out by IFCPF annually.

The Rules

Given the continuous cycle of annual modifications to the Laws and to avoid outdating this chapter before it is even published, it is best to describe the general rule modifications rather than specific ones to understand how CP football is played. It is also important to recognise that CP football is at different developmental stages for men's and women's competitions. Men have been playing CP football since the first match in Edinburgh, Scotland, in 1978, while women had their first international tournament in 2022.[46] To minimise the barriers that some countries may face in finding and recruiting enough players and funding the training needed to develop a women's programme, the game is played 5v5 with a 10-person roster, compared to the men's 7v7 format with a 14-person roster. The intent of IFCPF is to encourage more countries to start programmes, particularly during the early development stages of the women's CP football game.[45] This adjustment is intended to transition the women's game to the more traditional 7v7 format after allowing programmes opportunities to initiate and develop over the next 3–5 years. Consequently, the bulk of the rules will be described in the 7v7 format with some notation about how IFCPF has modified the game for the smaller 5v5 game.

Field and Equipment

As there are fewer players on the field of play, the ideal dimensions are 70 meters (+/– 3.5 meters) along the touchline and 50 meters (+/– 2.5 meters) along the goal line. Consequently, other parts of the field of play are made proportionately smaller, such as the penalty area (27 meters x 11 meters), the goal area (13 meters x 4 meters), the centre circle (7-meter radius) and the penalty mark (9 meters from the midpoint between the goalposts). The goal itself is 5 meters wide (inside of the posts) and 2 meters high (crossbar to the ground). Additionally, the minimum distance opposing players must be from free kicks is 7 meters, with additional rules for penalty kicks, indirect free kicks for the attacking team within seven meters of the goal line between the goal posts, or free kicks for the defensive team within their own penalty area.

The Players

In CP football, each team is permitted seven players on the field of play. Currently, there are 14 players on a roster, from which a maximum of five substitutes over three opportunities in time may be made in any match. If extra time is needed, each team may use an additional substitution and an additional opportunity, for a total of six substitutions and four opportunities.

As discussed in other chapters, classification is an important element of the CP football game. This is also reflected on the field of play with specific criteria that must be met regarding the various classifications of a team's players. Currently, there must be at least one FT1 class player, and only one FT3 player may be on the field from each team at any point in the game. If a team fails to have an FT1 player on the field, it must play short with a maximum of six players until an FT1 player joins or re-joins the match. This encourages teams to include individuals with a greater degree of eligible impairment on the field of play to best serve a broader range of athletes qualifying for the disability version of the game.

The Duration of the Match

As individuals with ambulatory CP tend to have lower levels of aerobic capacity compared to their peers without disabilities,[47] IFCPF has adopted 2 x 30-minute halves as the standard duration for a match with a 15-minute halftime. Should extra time be needed due to a competition requiring a winning team, an additional two periods of 10 minutes each are played. This is a change from the IFAB rules, which call for 2 x 45-minute halves, a 15-minute halftime, and, when required, two halves of extra time of 15 minutes each.

Determining the Outcome of a Match

Similar to the IFAB version of the game, if a game is tied after extra time and the competition requires a winner, IFCPF modifications outline that both teams would participate in a penalty shoot-out. In IFCPF, the number of kicks in the initial round is reduced from IFAB's recommended five kicks to three per team. If, at the end of each team's three kicks, the score is still level, kicks continue one at a time until one team scores more than the other after an equal number of kicks.

Offside

Perhaps the most important difference in the IFCPF game is that Law 11 (Offside) does not apply in CP football. While various changes to this modification have been proposed, such as the physical marking of offside lines on the field similar to the blue lines used in ice hockey, IFCPF has not implemented any offside element of the game thus far. In a 7v7 format, this encourages attacking play, allows for quick counterattacks and can challenge the goalkeeper, particularly on free-kick situations as having attacking players closer can increase obstruction of their line of sight to the ball. Existing offside modifications are elements of the game for which the IFCPF Referee and Technical Committees seek better understanding of their impacts on safe and fair play to determine whether further changes would be beneficial.

The Throw-In

Given the nature of players with cerebral palsy and the potential for bilateral or unilateral spasticity in their upper extremities, CP football permits players to choose between a traditional throw-in or rolling the ball into play. If they choose a traditional throw-in, they must abide by the procedures in IFAB's Law 15 without modification. If they choose to roll the ball into play, the ball may be released with one hand rather than both, but it must be rolled and touch the ground within 1 meter from the point of release. In both instances, opponents must remain 2 meters from the point of the touchline where the throw-in is taking place to allow for a proper restart, as required by IFAB's Law 15.

Figure 4.1 presents a compilation of the main adaptations to the rules of CP football in comparison to the IFAB rules.

The Women's Game

As previously mentioned, the women's game is played 5v5, at least for the next few years until more countries have had the opportunity to fully develop their squads. There are a few differences, which will be highlighted (see Figure 4.2).

The Field of Play

Since the game is played with five players per side, the field is smaller than the traditional 7v7 field. In this case, it is 40 meters by 27 meters, and the other dimensions are adjusted accordingly – the penalty area is 17 meters

Figure 4.1 A compilation of main adaptations to the CP football rules (for men).

by 9 meters, and the goal area is 9 meters by 4 meters. The goals themselves remain the same as in the 7v7 game.

Other modifications for the women's game include: opposing players needing to be 4 meters from free kicks (with additional rules when those free kicks are penalty kicks, indirect free kicks for the attacking team within 4 meters of the goal line between the goal posts, or free kicks for the defensive team within their own penalty area), two halves that are 25 minutes in length, and should a winner need to be determined, two halves of 8 minutes of extra time.

Figure 4.2 A compilation of main adaptations to the CP football rules (for women).

The Process of Becoming a CP Football Official

Having developed an understanding of the IFAB Laws of the Game and IFCPF Modifications to the IFAB Laws of the Game, it is also important to outline how one can become an official for CP football at the local, national and international levels.

IFCPF has designated a system for advancing as an official that outlines the requirements across eight levels. Levels 1 through 3 can be completed within the home country of the official, levels 4 and 5 are International level certifications, and levels 6 through 8 are Administrative levels of certification.

Level 1 involves referees becoming certified at the local level of IFAB referee training within their own country. Since IFAB is the foundation of the IFCPF game, a local certification as an IFAB official within one's own country is deemed as Level 1.

Level 2 certification involves an official's first formal interaction with IFCPF, requiring the completion of a two-hour online course delivered by the Coordinator of Education or Officiating Manager. This certification licenses participants to officiate CP football games in their communities or regions.

Level 3 certification can typically be obtained in one of two ways. First, for each IFCPF-sanctioned event, there is usually in-person training held in the host country prior to the event that provides the National level IFCPF certification. This training allows National CP football referees to officiate the IFCPF-sanctioned event, often serving as assistant referees. The second option is for an IFCPF region to host a virtual CP Football National Referee Training Course. This typically takes place over two evenings for 4+ hours of rules interpretation and video analysis, culminating in two tests. The first test assesses comprehension of the written Laws of the Game and IFCPF Modifications, while the second involves a video test evaluating the potential official's ability to interpret these Laws accurately in on-field decisions.

Upon completion of the Level 3 National certification, there are two opportunities for advancing to Level 4 National certification. The first is that officials interested in advancing to the International level and deemed qualified by their national football federation can be nominated for an upgrade by their home country. The second opportunity is earned by performing well at an IFCPF-sanctioned event as a National referee, leading to an invitation to upgrade.

Level 4 National certification is considered a provisional International Technical Official. Level 4 officials have increased responsibility at IFCPF-sanctioned events, must meet increased fitness demands and have a more thorough understanding of the Laws of the Game and IFCPF Modifications, as demonstrated in the classroom, during training sessions and on the field during games. Typically, only three to four officials are invited to become IFCPF Provisional International Technical Officials each year.

Should an individual perform very well at the Provisional level and demonstrate a commitment to the CP football game and community, they are appointed by the IFCPF Officiating Manager to become a ***Level 5*** International Technical Official (ITO) for the following year.

At the beginning of each calendar year, the Officiating Manager sends out an invitation to selected ITOs to certify or re-certify at that level for the year. Officials are asked to indicate how they have been staying active in CP football games at the local, national and international levels, as well as what games or leagues they are officiating using IFAB Laws. Officials must also upload the results of their most recent fitness test and their availability for the upcoming year's IFCPF events.

Level 6 marks the beginning of the Administration level for IFCPF Officials and is titled Competition Head of Officials. At each event, there must be one individual in charge of the officials who provides pre-competition training, makes officials' appointments for the event, evaluates officials' game performances and shares feedback, and reviews any protests that may arise from match incidents. This position is typically held by someone who has been an ITO for a significant amount of time and can support the development and growth of newer tournament officials.

Level 7 is the IFCPF Referee Education Coordinator. This individual is responsible for the development and coordination of the education programme within IFCPF. They work closely with the Officiating Manager and the Officiating Committee to implement various referee training programmes, determine points of emphasis in those training programmes for the upcoming year and assist in improving any elements of the IFCPF CP football game that may need support.

Finally, ***Level 8*** is the IFCPF Officiating Manager, who oversees all aspects of the IFCPF referee programmes, training, staffing and events. This individual, with support from the Referee Committee, is the only person who can appoint individuals as an ITO within the organisation as it is currently structured. They serve on the IFCPF Technical Committee and support the global development of the CP football game.

Conclusions and Practical Applications

The game of CP football is incredibly entertaining and allows players with neurological impairments to play the beautiful game. This is only possible because there are designated modifications to the Laws of the Game that allow the players to showcase their talents, along with a dedicated group of match officials who oversee the game and understand the nuances of these modifications. As the sport continues to evolve, so too will the modifications to the Laws of the Game. The goal of CP football, both now and in the future, is that at each event, the talent and skill of these remarkable players can be put on display. The Laws of the Game, the IFCPF Modifications to the IFAB Laws of the Game and the officials making on-field decisions based on these Laws are all integral to achieving this goal.

5 Eligibility and Classification

Matías Henríquez and Raúl Reina

Contextual Framework

Classification serves as the framework for Para sports, enabling individuals with disabilities to compete at high-performance levels by minimising the impact of impairments on athletic outcomes.[48] Broadly, classification regulates and controls the matching of competitors based on inequalities, specifically addressing the impact of eligible impairments (see Figure 5.1) on specific skills.[49] This system relies on identifying various eligible impairment types and assessing the degree of activity limitation, in accordance with the guidelines of the ICF, which classifies health domains in humans.[48] Classification systems define the minimum impairment required for participation in Para sport competitions, grouping athletes with disabilities into different sport classes to ensure fair competition and that success is determined by sporting excellence.[50] Thus, fair classification systems are crucial for the integrity of Para sports and the equitable participation of athletes with various impairments.[51]

In this context, the role of the IPC is pivotal. The IPC established a Classification Code that provides guidelines for all Para sports included in the Paralympic Games programme or aspiring to be included. A new Classification Code will be implemented from 1 January 2025, with purposes summarised as follows[52]:

To enable athletes with eligible impairments to participate in competitive Para sport with a pathway to sporting excellence, culminating in the Paralympic Games.

To establish a unique framework that promotes fair and meaningful competition by minimising the impact of athletes' impairments on competition outcomes, ensuring that success is determined by factors other than impairment.

To fulfil two critical functions: 1) determining which athletes are eligible to compete in Para sport; and 2) grouping eligible athletes into sport classes based on the extent to which their impairments affect their ability to perform specific tasks and activities fundamental to the sport.

DOI: 10.4324/9781032708942-5

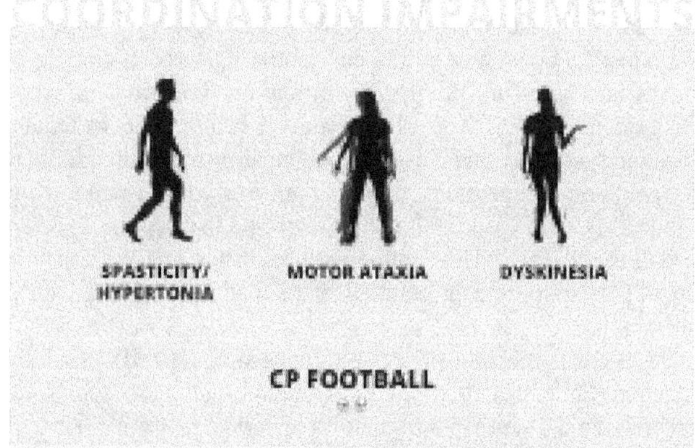

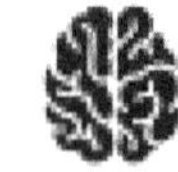

Figure 5.1 Eligible impairments for the IPC and for playing CP football (IFCPF) (adapted from IFCPF, 2023).[45]

Para sport classification systems are designed to group athletes based on the impact of their impairments, not their sport performance. An athlete's classification is based on the extent to which their impairment affects their ability to perform fundamental activities in their specific sport. Improved performance within a sport class does not warrant a change in sport class.

Under the new IPC Classification Code, seven eligible impairments are considered (five physical, one visual and one intellectual). For CP football, eligibility is restricted to those with Coordination Impairments (i.e., the ability to voluntarily produce skilled movement fluidly, rapidly and accurately).[53] This includes having one or more of the following three movement disorders that (1) adversely affect the ability to voluntarily produce a full range of skilled movement fluidly, rapidly and accurately and (2) are consistent with an underlying health condition (e.g., CP, TBI or stroke) affecting the central nervous system:

a) *Hypertonia/Spasticity*: an increase in muscle tension that may be velocity-dependent and/or a reduced ability of a muscle to stretch.
b) *Motor Ataxia*: limited precision in the direction and velocity of voluntary movement.
c) *Dyskinesia (athetosis, dystonia, chorea)*: involuntary movements that interfere with voluntary movements.

The IPC mandates the development of evidence-based classification practices, including valid measures of impairments using empirical evidence to allocate athletes into sports classes.[2] The classification process involves several stages to assess athletes' impairments and activity limitations, initially assigning a provisional class that is later confirmed or adjusted based on competition observation. All methods used must be valid, reliable and based on the best available evidence regarding the impact of the impairment on sports performance.[48] This approach stems from the origins of the Paralympic movement and the rehabilitation of individuals with disabilities.[54]

From the inception of Para sport, classification systems have evolved through three distinct stages: medical-based approaches, functional systems and evidence-based classification systems.[55] From a historical perspective, since athletes with CP were first included in the Paralympic Games in 1980 and the inaugural international CP football competition in 1978, medical diagnoses have been employed to allocate participants with neurological conditions.[55] Over time, the focus shifted from rehabilitation to sport-specific performance, resulting in functional systems that emphasise the impact of impairments on performance.[56] These functional systems represented a significant advancement by considering the practical implications of impairments on athletic performance rather than solely relying on medical diagnoses. The most recent stage, evidence-based classification systems, builds upon this foundation by utilising empirical research to validate the classification process. This approach ensures that classification not only reflects the athletes' impairments but also how these impairments affect their ability to perform in their sport. This shift towards evidence-based practices underscores the importance of fairness and accuracy in the classification process, promoting competitive equity and enhancing the integrity of Para sports.

CP Football Classification

CP football is a team Para sport that mirrors the multiple intermittent physical demands of its able-bodied counterpart but includes modifications to facilitate the participation of individuals with neurological impairments.[57] These modifications, essential to ensure fair competition, are primarily guided by the classification system, which categorises participants based on eligible impairments affecting coordination due to neurological issues.[58] The current classification system is divided into four main stages:[56]

Assessment of Impairment Structure and Function: This involves evaluating reflexes, muscle spasticity and range of movement.

Activity Limitation in Critical Motor Tasks: This stage assesses limitations in essential motor tasks specific to the sport, such as running, jumping and changing direction.

Evaluation of Activity Limitation in Sport-Specific Tasks: This includes tasks like dribbling the ball, shooting and participating in small-sided games.

Assessment of Contextual Factors and Other Impairments: This considers factors such as training level, age and anthropometry that may contribute to activity limitations.

All these stages are necessary for providing a sports class allocation and status, which are recorded in a master list provided by the IFCPF (Figure 5.2).

With the new 2025 IPC Classification Code, these stages will be readjusted over a two-year period as follows:

Part I: *Underlying Health Condition (UHC) Assessment.*

Stage 1: UHC Assessment to verify that the athlete has (or has had) at least one medically and/or clinically diagnosed UHC, based on a review of Diagnostic Information provided by the Athlete's National Federation.

Part II: *Evaluation Session.*

Stage 2: Eligible Impairment Assessment to confirm that the athlete has an eligible impairment catered for by the sport that is consistent with one or more UHCs reported in Stage 1, and that there are no inconsistencies with such reported UHC(s).

Figure 5.2 Athlete classification stages of the CP football process (adapted from IFCPF, 2023).[45]

Stage 3: Minimum Impairment Criteria (MIC) Assessment to determine whether the athlete's eligible impairment meets the applicable MIC for that impairment within CP football.

Stage 4: Sport Class Assessment, consisting of: 1) Allocating a sport class based on an assessment of the extent to which the athlete's eligible impairment(s) impact their ability to execute the specific tasks and activities fundamental to CP football; 2) Assigning a sport class status to indicate whether and when the athlete may be required to undergo classification in the future.

Remarkably, evidence-based practices have been described considering valid and reliable protocols that permit the identification of differences between profiles, thereby favouring the allocation of athletes' sports classes. A significant volume of scientific literature supports procedures to classify athletes with coordination impairments, considering the evaluation of impairments[59, 60] and certain relevant activity limitations,[61–65] and their association with sports performance, as shown in Table 5.1.[66, 67]

The evolution of classification systems has significantly impacted CP football participation frameworks, transitioning towards functional approaches that organise athletes based on the type of impairment, such as bilateral spasticity or diplegia (FT5 sport class), ataxia or athetosis (FT6), unilateral spasticity or hemiplegia (FT7) and minimal impairment with any of the aforementioned profiles (FT8). Initially, the classification system in CP football allowed for significant performance variations due to a cut-point problem in the allocation of sport classes, which could result in different possible

Table 5.1 Different physical assessments to evaluate players during the CP football classification system.

Impairment Assessment	*Activity Limitation*	*Sport-Specific Activity Limitation*
Neurological reflex activity	Rapid Heel-Toe; Split Jumps; Side-Step	10 m Sprint Test with Ball
Modified Ashworth scale	Triple Hop Test; Standing Broad Jump; Four Bounds for Distance	Dribbling Speed Test; 505 Test with Ball
Selective Control Assessment of the Lower Extremity (SCALE)	One-Leg Stance; Countermovement Jump	Small Sided-Game (i.e., 2 vs 2)
Scale for the Assessment and Rating of Ataxia (SARA)	10 m Sprint Test	Specific Field Player Technical Assessment
Dyskinesia Impairment Scale (DIS)	Modified Agility Test; 505 Test	Specific Goalkeeper Technical Assessment

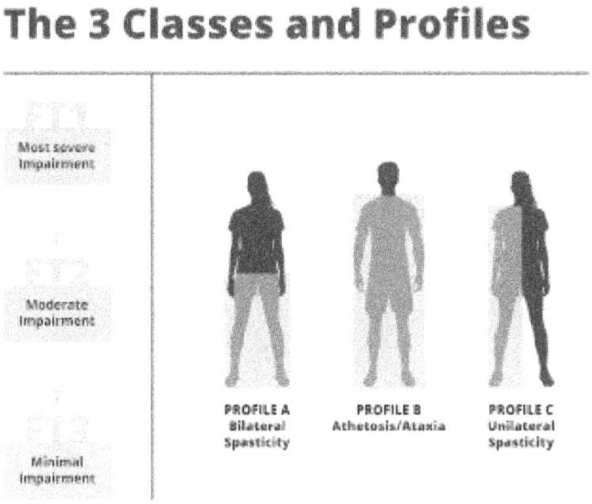

Figure 5.3 Sport classes and physical profiles for CP football (adapted from IFCPF, 2023).[45]

classifications (e.g., FT5 or FT8 for moderate or mild spastic diplegia, FT6 or FT8 for moderate or mild athetosis or ataxia, FT7 or FT8 for moderate or mild spastic hemiplegia, and FT8 or Not Eligible when mild profiles meet the MIC or not, respectively).

In 2018, after a six-year research period, the CP football classification system evolved to address this issue, moving towards evidence-based approaches that employ reliable testing to allow classifiers to accurately distinguish sports classes and use reference data to inform decision-making.[68] Figure 5.3 schematically represents the current classification system, organised by the impairment profile of para-footballers (A = bilateral spasticity, B = athetosis/dystonia (dyskinesia) or ataxia, C = unilateral spasticity) and the severity level of these impairments, as well as the activity limitation on fundamental motor and football skills (1 = severe involvement, 2 = moderate involvement or 3 = mild involvement). Thus, FT1 and FT3 sports classes include para-footballers with the highest and lowest levels of impairment and activity limitation, respectively.[69] According to technical rules, at least one player class FT1 must be on the field at all times, and a maximum of only one player FT3 is allowed to play during the game, factors that influence participation rates and team configurations.[45]

Evidence-Based Classification in CP Football

The current classification system for CP football is constructed using a combination of quantitative and qualitative methods to assess players, aligning with evidence-based practices and the current IPC Classification Code. From 1980 to 2015, CP football was governed by the CPISRA. Since then, it has transitioned to being overseen by the IFCPF. Since the first IPC Classification Code of 2007, CP football has continuously improved classification operations, pioneering research and evidence-based methods for para-athletes with coordination impairments.

The CP football classification committee, along with other organisational members, collaborators and para-athletes, has made significant efforts to meet the requirements of the IPC Code. These efforts have resulted in extensive research and academic work supporting the classification system, translating this knowledge into practical methods for class allocation of para-footballers. Following the research requirements for developing evidence-based classification systems, as outlined by Tweedy et al.,[68] the process can be detailed as follows:

Step 1: Identify Impairment Types and Assess Performance Determinants

Reina[56] explored the eligible impairments for CP football, emphasising the importance of assessing performance determinants to develop a classification system that accurately places para-athletes into appropriate sport classes based on the extent of activity limitation caused by their impairments. The classification system aims to ensure that competitive success within a sport class is determined by factors such as skill, determination and training, rather than the severity of the impairment. By considering impairments that impact activities specific to football, such as passing, running and changing direction, the classification system aims to minimise the impact of impairment on competition outcomes. Research has been conducted to develop specific measurements of impairment that reduce potential subjective bias, diminish the clinical-specific approach covered by the new UHC Assessment and create impairment measurements resistant to training while also transferable to the skills required for sports performance.

Step 2: Develop Valid, Standardised, Sport-Specific Measures of Impairment and Performance

Previous works have described the theoretical model of the classification system in this team Para sport and the principal determinants of sports performance in CP football, aligning with international requirements.[56] Additionally, CP football has developed opportunities for feedback from the sports community on the development of an evidence-based classification system.[70] Early studies have supported the development of standardised, sport-specific measures of performance determinants related to change of direction, vertical and horizontal jump, acceleration/deceleration, sprint capacity and technical aspects of the sport, which help differentiate between FT5 and FT8 sport classes.[59, 71–73]

Step 3: Identify Measures of Impairment that Account for a Significant and Independent Portion of the Variance in Performance

In the classification of para-footballers with CP, several measures of impairment significantly and independently explain the variance in performance. Pastor et al.[74] developed a mathematical model aiding decision-making based on the severity of coordination impairments, which was crucial for classifying athletes effectively. Reina et al.[60] emphasised the importance of both dynamic and static stability, correlating these with specific impairment profiles to better understand performance outcomes. Additionally, Reina et al.[64] highlighted how the inclusion of a ball affects change of direction and sprint tests, providing valuable insights for evidence-based classification. Further, Roldan et al.[59] investigated limb spasticity's impact on motor performance, demonstrating its substantial influence on athletic capabilities. Lastly, Sarabia et al.[75] and Yanci et al.[76] employed decision trees and comparative match loads respectively, to refine classifiers' decision-making processes regarding activity limitations and performance metrics among para-footballers. These studies collectively underscore the multifaceted nature of impairment measures, each contributing uniquely to the comprehensive understanding of performance variance in CP football.

Step 4: Develop Minimum Impairment Criteria and Classes Based on Measures of Impairment that Are Significantly Associated with Performance

Identifying the relationships between impairment and sports performance is particularly challenging in team Paralympic sports due to multiple performance factors. However, research in CP football suggests that the relationship between coordination impairments and sports performance may be impairment-specific.[59, 60, 67] Additionally, high-quality research studies have validated different decision-making algorithms to provide classifiers with data-driven, objective recommendations, minimising individual classifier bias.[74, 75]

Pastor et al.[74] proposed a mathematical model to guide classification decisions based on coordination impairments. Reina et al.[60] identified a relationship between impaired coordination and match physical load, underscoring the necessity of considering these factors for accurate classification. Further research by Reina et al.[67] highlighted the importance of activity limitation and match load as crucial metrics for evidence-based classification. Additionally, Roldan et al.[59] demonstrated the substantial impact of limb spasticity on motor performance, reinforcing the need for its inclusion in impairment criteria. These findings collectively support the development of robust, evidence-based classification systems in CP football.

Further Challenges and Steps in CP Football Classification: 2025 IPC Classification Code and Point-Based System

The classification of CP football is currently navigating several challenges as it strives to comply with the new 2025 IPC Classification Code. One significant issue is the creation of new profiles to address the cut-point problem in the current classification system. The diversity of profiles and the varying impact of impairments on CP footballers result in some players falling into a borderline zone, where their profiles do not fit neatly into the existing classes. To address this, efforts are underway to describe this grey zone, potentially leading to the creation of two new profiles: FT1.5, for players between FT1 and FT2, and FT2.5, for players between FT2 and FT3. Consequently, a new technical rule should be adopted to determine the maximum points allowed to sum all the seven players on the field of play.

The IFCPF must ensure alignment with the new IPC Classification Code, meeting international standards and strengthening compliance. This includes implementing a new classifier training and certification process. Continuous improvement in classifier reliability and the practical application of research based on evidence-based practices are crucial. Significant efforts have been made to quantitatively assess impairments such as motor ataxia, athetosis or dystonia, all of which traditionally involve qualitative assessments that need enhancement. However, assessing para-athletes with these impairments remains an ongoing challenge for the entire Paralympic movement.

Conclusions and Practical Applications

Classification in Para sports such as CP football emerged to ensure fair competition by categorising para-athletes based on the impact of their impairments on specific sport skills. Over time, this system has transitioned from medical-based approaches to functional systems and now to an evidence-based framework, emphasising the relationship between impairments and sports performance. The current classification system, managed by the IFCPF under IPC guidelines, rigorously assesses impairments such as spasticity, dyskinesia and motor ataxia, using standardised tests to evaluate fundamental football skills like running, jumping, changing direction and dribbling.

This approach not only categorises para-athletes into specific sport classes but also ensures competitive integrity and fairness through empirical validation and research-backed methodologies. Challenges remain, particularly with the new 2025 IPC Classification Code, which addresses a new 'cut-point problem' to better accommodate para-athletes whose impairments fall between existing sport classes. To address this issue, efforts are underway to describe the grey zone, potentially leading to the creation of new profiles, such as FT1.5 and FT2.5, and necessitating the adoption of new technical rules to determine the maximum points allowed for the seven players on the field.

Despite these challenges, ongoing efforts in research and classification methodology continue to enhance the accuracy and fairness of CP football classification. The IFCPF must ensure alignment with the new IPC Classification Code, including the implementation of a new classifier training and certification process. Continuous improvement in classifier reliability and the practical application of evidence-based practices are crucial. Significant efforts have been made to quantitatively assess impairments such as motor ataxia, athetosis and dystonia, which have traditionally involved qualitative assessments needing enhancement.

In conclusion, the evolution of the classification system has significantly impacted CP football, transitioning towards functional and evidence-based approaches that organise athletes based on the type and severity of impairments. The ongoing efforts to refine the classification system, including the introduction of new profiles and the enhancement of impairment assessments, are vital steps in addressing current challenges and aligning with the new IPC Classification Code. These advancements will contribute to a more accurate and fair classification process, ultimately enhancing the competitive experience for para-athletes in CP football and supporting the sport's growth and the participation of athletes with diverse neurological conditions.

6 Physical and Physiological Responses during Competition

Javier Yanci, Aitor Iturricastillo, Matías Henríquez and Daniel Castillo

Contextual Framework

In any team sport, it is essential to analyse the physical and psychophysiological demands of the competition to understand the game requirements. Specifically in regular football, this analysis enables coaches and physical conditioning trainers to: (1) periodise the training sessions of the season, (2) improve post-competition recovery methods, and (3) adjust post-match week training strategies, among other decisive factors for physical performance.[77] Similarly, in a team para-sport such as CP football, knowledge of these factors is beneficial for coaches and physical trainers. In recent years, there has been an increased volume of research on the physical and psychophysiological demands of CP football matches at international and national levels.[69] This descriptive data has provided coaches and physical trainers with valuable information to prepare matches optimally and to manage post-competition recovery for players with neuromuscular impairments, whose profiles differ from those of able-bodied footballers.

When analysing the sport discipline of football for people with CP, it is important to consider the considerable differences compared to conventional football (as seen in Chapters 4 and 5): the dimensions of the pitch (70 m × 50 m), playing time (two halves of 30 minutes), the number of players (7-a-side) and a sport classification system that determines who can compete. To participate in CP football, players must have a permanent neurological impairment, such as hypertonia, ataxia or athetosis, affecting their performance and skills. These impairments, caused by conditions such as congenital CP or acquired brain injury, must meet minimum eligibility criteria. Eligible players are classified into three sport classes (FT1 = severe, FT2 = moderate, FT3 = mild) based on the impact on their abilities. All these variables must be considered when analysing the descriptive data provided by the different studies on this specific para-athlete population.

This chapter provides relevant information about the physical and psychophysiological responses of CP footballers during official matches. This information will enable coaches and physical trainers to periodise the season,

DOI: 10.4324/9781032708942-6

plan post-competition recovery methods and adjust post-match week training strategies, among other important factors.

Physical Responses Quantification in CP Football Competition

The physical responses of football players with CP have been defined as the amount of work performed, referring to physical measures such as distance covered, distance covered at different running intensities or the number of actions at different intensities.[76] In this context, the competition's physical responses encompass all those physical indicators that quantitatively and qualitatively reflect the work performed during the match, similar to what has been investigated in able-bodied footballers.

In recent decades, technological advancements have allowed for a deeper understanding of these responses and have enabled the collection of reliable and relatively straightforward competition information. Existing technology currently allows for the quantification of the physical responses of football players, primarily using optical motion systems, global positioning systems (GPS) and local positioning systems (LPS).[78] Notably, a significant number of recent studies in CP football have utilised GPS technology due to its higher accessibility and growing popularity in the world of football.[69] GPS devices provide information regarding specific physical and positional responses, with players wearing a specific vest that has a pocket, usually placed on the back, where a compact-sized apparatus is inserted. This device connects to various satellites, allowing for real-time tracking of the player and providing information about their position, movement, speed, movement patterns and player load metrics.[79]

In football players with CP, using models and variables applied to able-bodied footballers as examples, several indicators of physical responses have been analysed, including:

a) Total distance covered.
b) Distance covered at different running intensities.
c) Highest achieved speed.
d) Number and magnitude of accelerations and decelerations.
e) Number, magnitude and orientation of changes of direction.
f) Global load indicators such as player load (PL) or metabolic power, both described in absolute values and relative to match duration or player participation during matches.

Table 6.1 presents the most commonly used variables in quantifying physical responses in CP football players, along with results obtained in different studies as examples.

Table 6.1 Physical responses in official matches by CP elite footballers obtained from different studies.

	Yanci et al., 2019 (Absolute values)	*Yanci et al., 2018 (Relative values)*	*Reina et al., 2021 (Relative values)*	*Reina et al. 2020 (Relative values)*	*Yanci et al., 2022 (Relative values)*
TD (m or m/min)	4342.7 ± 1808.4	92.63 ± 13.54	–	84.51 ± 16.50	84.94 ± 15.99
Velmax (km/h)	22.7 ± 2.3	22.81 ± 2.34	22.95 ± 2.01	22.58 ± 3.18	22.50 ± 3.04
Distance at different intensities (m or m/min)					
LW (< 0.4 km/h)	56.6 ± 49.3	1.11 ± 0.68	–	2.68 ± 1.21	3.16 ± 18.54
W (0.4–3.0 km/h)	408.7 ± 363.9	8.30 ± 4.93	–	10.16 ± 5.03	10.39 ± 5.29
J (3.0–9.0 km/h)	1920.0 ± 821.1	40.02 ± 4.84	–	42.33 ± 8.52	41.86 ± 7.71
MIR (9.0–13.0 km/h)	1270.3 ± 600.0	27.87 ± 9.18	–	19.38 ± 25.45	18.05 ± 7.49
HIR (13.0–18.0 km/h)	537.6 ± 283.4	12.00 ± 4.52	11.87 ± 4.71	9.47 ± 5.46	9.56 ± 5.52
SPR (> 18.0 km/h)	148.0 ± 97.4	3.27 ± 1.96	3.38 ± 2.01	3.05 ± 2.79	3.17 ± 2.99
Short-term actions (number or number/min)					
Moderate Acc (1.0/2.78 m/s2)	50.1 ± 37.6	1.06 ± 0.58	0.98 ± 0.50	5.55 ± 3.81	5.33 ± 4.39
High Acc (> 2.78 m/s2)	3.5 ± 3.2	0.07 ± 0.07	0.07 ± 0.07	1.08 ± 0.66	1.03 ± 0.73
Moderate Dec (−1.0/−2.78 m/s2)	49.7 ± 33.4	1.03 ± 0.47	0.95 ± 0.42	4.49 ± 3.15	4.245 ± 3.20
High Dec (> −2.78 m/s2)	5.7 ± 4.3	0.12 ± 0.09	0.11 ± 0.08	0.76 ± 0.72	0.70 ± 0.64
PL (AU or AU/min)	487.6 ± 214.2	10.56 ± 2.19	10.49 ± 2.28	9.85 ± 2.26	9.94 ± 2.17
PMP (watt or watt/min)	112.3 ± 37.0	113.21 ± 36.94	115.16 ± 38.04	–	–
Low intensity COD (number/min)					
Forward	29.6 ± 24.2	0.62 ± 0.38	–	–	–
Back	44.2 ± 26.1	0.94 ± 0.41	–	–	–
Left	121.7 ± 73.7	2.64 ± 1.82	–	–	–
Right	150.1 ± 89.2	3.27 ± 1.73	–	–	–
Medium intensity COD (number/min)					
Forward	8.4 ± 6.2	0.17 ± 0.10	–	–	–
Back	16.4 ± 10.9	0.34 ± 0.17	–	–	–
Left	19.8 ± 14.2	0.42 ± 0.24	–	–	–
Right	23.6 ± 13.7	0.52 ± 0.26	–	–	–

(*Continued*)

Table 6.1 (Continued)

	Yanci et al., 2019 (Absolute values)	*Yanci et al., 2018 (Relative values)*	*Reina et al., 2021 (Relative values)*	*Reina et al. 2020 (Relative values)*	*Yanci et al., 2022 (Relative values)*
High intensity COD (number/min)					
Forward	4.1 ± 3.2	0.09 ± 0.07	–	–	–
Back	6.9 ± 5.5	0.14 ± 0.11	–	–	–
Left	5.6 ± 5.8	0.11 ± 0.11	–	–	–
Right	6.3 ± 4.4	0.13 ± 0.09	–	–	–

TD = total distance, Velmax = maximum velocity, LW = Low walking, W = Walking, J = Jogging, MIR = Medium Intensity Running, HIR = High Intensity Running, SPR = Sprinting. Acc = acceleration, Dec = deceleration, COD = changes of direction, AU = arbitrary units.

In addition to describing the physical responses during competition, several studies have focused on analysing the effects of various contextual variables that may impact players' physical responses. Regarding functional class, it has been observed that physical responses vary among different sport classes.[57, 76] Most studies suggest that players in FT1 classes have lower physical responses than those in FT2 and FT3 in variables relevant to sports performance. Similarly, it has been noted that FT3 class players, who present minimal impairment impact, exhibit the highest physical responses.[60, 67] Recent research has also observed that players' impairments are associated with their physical responses in competition, an aspect particularly relevant to sports classification in para-sports.

Moreover, a recent study has observed differences in players' physical responses based on the altitude above sea level where matches are played.[69] Differences and associations in physical responses between official and friendly matches have also been analysed,[80] as well as between full matches and reduced games. The impact of playing multiple consecutive matches and the competitive level of teams and players have also been investigated, revealing a different performance pattern characterised by the neuromuscular characteristics of these football players.[66, 81]

Psychophysiological Responses Quantification in CP Football Competition

A deeper understanding of the demands of CP football competition necessitates quantifying not only the physical responses but also the psychophysiological responses of the players. Athletes may experience different physiological loads in response to the same physical effort or external load due to their individual anthropometric, physical, physiological or psychological characteristics. This knowledge provides relevant information for designing training strategies and facilitates the planning and periodisation of training sessions. Consequently, the coaching staff can apply appropriate training doses, thereby helping players to minimise their risk of injury. The training process is based on the relationship between the psychophysiological responses generated in the body and the proposed training stimulus. Accordingly, measures of internal load can be indicators reflecting the actual psychophysiological response that the body initiates to cope with the physical demands. Both objective and subjective methods are used in the scientific literature to quantify these responses.

In this context, heart rate (HR) is an objective method that has become the most widely used variable for recording internal load and training intensity.[82] This indicator, together with heart rate variability (HRV), provides insight into the state of the autonomic nervous system and the level of aerobic fitness.[83] Additionally, this record allows strength and conditioning specialists to understand the time spent in different training zones and estimate the load that the competition has placed on the athlete. On the other hand, the literature presents other subjective methods used in conventional football such as rated perceived exertion (RPE),[84] perceived fatigue, well-being state and recovery status, among others, to quantify psychophysiological stress.

Unfortunately, studies focused on understanding the psychophysiological responses encountered by CP footballers have primarily addressed HR responses and perceived efforts. For example, maximum HR values range from 200 ± 6 to 173 ± 28 bpm, and mean HR values range from 153 ± 19 to 171 ± 7 bpm.[81, 85] These values are similar to those shown by able-bodied footballers, with maximum HR values of 200 ± 11 bpm and mean HR values of 158 ± 10 bpm.[86] Since only one study presents the results according to sport class, more research is necessary to analyse this aspect. Interestingly, when a specific analysis is conducted comparing the physiological demands based on the nature of the competition, international competitions exhibit higher maximum and mean HR values (200 ± 6 and 171 ± 7 bpm, respectively) compared to national competitions (194 ± 13 and 154 ± 22 bpm, respectively).[81, 85] Moreover, only one study explored HRV, suggesting improvements in this parameter after one week of football training in Brazilian players with CP.[87]

Regarding the use of RPE metrics, only two studies have been published on Chilean footballers with CP. These studies reported a mean of 6.3 ± 1.5 points on the RPE scale and a match load of 370 ± 89 AU in the Chilean Football League of CP football. This study did not find significant differences ($p > 0.05$) in the RPE indicators according to sport class and playing position. In another investigation, 14 international Chilean CP footballers of the national team compared a simulated game played 7-a-side with two small-sided game drills played 2-a-side and 4-a-side. The authors found significant differences in RPE, with drills involving fewer players generating higher levels of exertion, similar to what has been reported in regular football.[69]

Conclusions and Practical Applications

In summary, understanding the physical and psychophysiological demands of CP football is crucial for coaches and trainers to optimise training and recovery strategies, considering the unique challenges posed by footballers with CP. This chapter emphasises the significance of the use of technological advancements, particularly GPS technology, in quantifying and understanding the match-running performance of football players with hypertonia, ataxia or athetosis. The accessibility and popularity of GPS devices have facilitated comprehensive analyses of various indicators, including total distance covered, running intensities, speed, accelerations, decelerations, changes of direction and global load indicators. Moreover, the exploration of contextual factors offers valuable insights into the diverse physical responses observed among players in different playing/training scenarios. Heart rate and subjective measures are crucial indicators aiding training/competition strategy design, but more research on psychophysiological responses in CP footballers is needed. This comprehensive knowledge equips professionals to enhance performance, periodise training and refine post-match strategies for footballers with CP.

To enhance the understanding of CP football, future research could examine performance metrics, recovery strategies and psychological aspects specific to each level such as comparing the national versus international level. In addition, exploring how contextual factors and rehabilitation impact access to CP football will shed light on inclusivity challenges, potentially uncovering ways to enhance participation. Investigating women's CP football involvement is crucial for gender-specific insights, addressing the unique challenges and opportunities that female players face. Moreover, understanding neuromuscular fatigue in players with different CP subtypes (spasticity, ataxia, athetosis) can guide tailored training programmes for optimal performance and injury prevention. Lastly, as was presented in this chapter, more research is needed to comprehensively grasp CP footballers' physical and physiological responses, in which prioritised collaborative efforts can bridge gaps in current knowledge.

7 Technical and Tactical Requirements

Stuart Sharp, Kai Lammert and Matías Henríquez

Contextual Framework

Football, a game characterised by its intricate tasks within a dynamic and unpredictable system, requires players to constantly adapt to changing situations while making split-second decisions in pursuit of scoring goals.[88] Similarly, CP football shares some characteristics with its mainstream counterpart, particularly in the principles of field-based invasion sports concerning technical and tactical actions. However, despite these parallels, CP football possesses unique attributes that distinguish individual and collective performance, such as the neuromuscular characteristics of players, game rules and the classification structure.[89]

CP football is rapidly gaining popularity and practice worldwide, promoting participation in competitive events for both male and female players of different ages and at various levels.[58] This surge in interest aligns with the increasing professionalism of participating teams across various competitions, accompanied by a wealth of available information about the sport.[89–91]

The technical and tactical aspects of regular football are well-studied, with a considerable volume of literature describing the key components of successful performance amidst the complex interactions during matches.[92] Many of these technical and tactical concepts apply to CP football, albeit with necessary adjustments to accommodate the unique characteristics and skill levels of individuals with CP. Despite the limited volume of literature on the topic, this chapter will review some of the main technical and tactical characteristics of CP football, addressing contextual factors relevant to understanding the dynamics of this discipline. Furthermore, practical guidance on training technical football skills and tactical behaviours in CP football will be provided, offering coaches a valuable starting point for their coaching endeavours.

Technical Characteristics of Football Players with CP

Players with CP exhibit a range of abilities and strategies to adapt to the technical demands of football. This section categorises players based on the class

DOI: 10.4324/9781032708942-7

and severity of impairment (i.e., FT1 to FT3) and the topography of involvement (i.e., bilateral spasticity, coordination impairments, unilateral spasticity), using the framework established by the IFCPF. It is essential for practitioners and coaches to recognise that each player possesses unique capabilities, and significant discrepancies may exist between players with the same class and profile. This variability must be considered when designing technical training sessions to help footballers identify the optimal positioning and strategies for playing with the ball. The severity of impairment influences the degree of difficulty in mastering football technical skills, although key features can be identified for specific topographical profiles.[64] Tailoring technical training to individual needs enables players to optimise their positioning and playing strategies.

Bilateral Spasticity

Players with bilateral spasticity (e.g., spastic diplegia) exhibit involvement in both legs, often experiencing decreased stride length and fatigue, which can affect sprinting, changing direction, dribbling, long passing and shooting.[72] Severe diplegic patterns and high muscle tone may lead to rotational abnormalities and pelvic misalignment, prompting players to contact the ball with the external surface of the foot.[93] Training for these players should focus on enhancing basic motor skills and optimising functionality, considering the impact of the impairment and leveraging potential football resources for performance.

Unilateral Spasticity

Unilateral spasticity (e.g., spastic hemiplegia) is one of the most prevalent profiles among footballers with CP.[75] These players typically rely on their dominant side, with minimal use of the affected side due to neurological impairments, resulting in significant asymmetries and performance discrepancies between the legs.[58, 63] Through training and technique optimisation, incorporating the non-dominant leg, players can develop efficient movement strategies for ball control, passing and turning. They also learn to position themselves on the field to minimise the impact of the impaired side, dribbling with the dominant side and covering the ball effectively with both sides. Coaches should instruct teammates to pass the ball to the dominant side, facilitating ball movement and providing passing options. Understanding teammates' impairments is crucial for optimising technical performance.

Coordination Impairments

Players with coordination impairments, such as ataxia, dystonia or athetosis, face challenges in coordination, stability and power, which are critical aspects of football performance.[71] Spatio-temporal coordination issues can hinder proficiency in controlling aerial balls, accelerating or decelerating during dribbling (see Figure 7.1) and making multiple adjustments for shooting. These players often require more space and time during both defensive and attacking actions. Training should focus on optimising the player's functionality, considering the permanent activity limitations caused by neural impairments.

Tactical Aspects of CP Football

In CP football, game models, styles of play and tactical strategies closely resemble those of regular football, albeit with adjustments to account for the unique nature of the sport.[88] Players' participation in CP football is determined by their classification profile and proficiency. Players with severe impairments (i.e., FT1) and a lower classification profile are often strategically placed as goalkeepers or attackers, leveraging the sport's no-offside rule and considering the game's high physical demands.[89] Due to mobility challenges, some coaches position players with severe impairments as goalkeepers, capitalising on the smaller goalpost dimensions and the specialised demands of the position. Despite motor difficulties, players adapt over time, enabling them to compete at elite levels. Alternatively, coaches may exploit the absence of the offside rule by deploying players with severe impairments as attackers near the opponent's goal. This tactic can disrupt the opposing team's defensive setup, creating space for midfielders.

Figure 7.1 Picture of a player with right unilateral spasticity. Photo courtesy of the IFCPF.

Players with moderate impairments (i.e., FT2 class) are most abundant on the field, fulfilling various roles within the team structure. These players compose the main structures of teams, with tactical positioning varying according to the needs of each team. Players with mild impairments (i.e., FT3 class) are highly valuable, often serving as midfielders or attackers due to their physical prowess and technical proficiency.[45] A small number of FT3-classified players act as goalkeepers, possibly because coaches prefer to use these versatile players in field actions, taking advantage of their ability to play effectively with both limbs.[89]

In CP football, coaches can choose offensive and defensive styles of play based on the characteristics of their team and various factors influencing performance. Tactics are tailored to the realities of CP football, with coaches employing systems such as defensive, offensive and possession strategies. These strategies are implemented through the use of different playing systems, based on the initial positions of the players on the pitch, and assigning specific roles to each player according to their position within the system. The most commonly used playing systems in CP football are as follows (see Figure 7.2):

1-3-3 System

The 1-3-3 system in 7-a-side football features 1 goalkeeper, 3 defenders and 3 midfielders, with no specific forwards. This system prioritises a solid defence and a robust midfield, providing balance and control in the centre of the pitch. The advantages include good defensive coverage and control of the game in the midfield, ideal for maintaining possession and building attacks from the midfield. However, this system may lack depth in attack, which could make

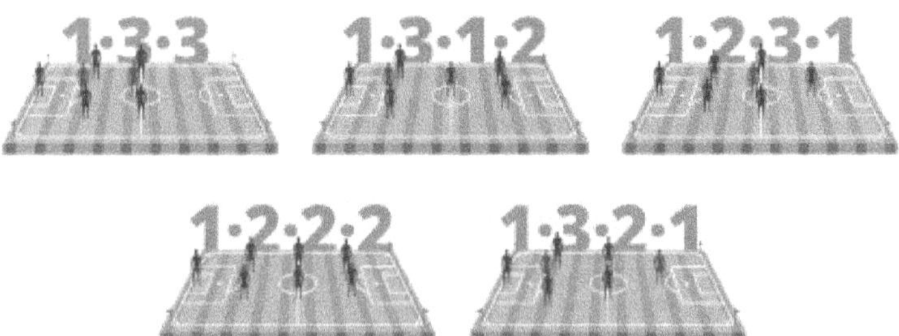

Figure 7.2 Representation of most commonly used playing systems in CP football.

creating clear goal-scoring opportunities difficult, and it requires the midfielders to constantly support both defence and attack.

1-3-2-1 System

In the 1-3-2-1 system, the team is arranged with 1 goalkeeper, 3 defenders, 2 midfielders and 1 forward. This system offers a combination of defensive solidity with a centralised offensive presence. The advantages include defensive stability and the possibility of a focused attack through the forward, making it useful for teams that seek to counter-attack quickly. However, it can leave the midfield vulnerable against teams with a more populated midfield and requires a highly effective and self-sufficient forward.

1-3-1-2 System

The 1-3-1-2 system comprises 1 goalkeeper, 3 defenders, 1 midfielder and 2 forwards. This system emphasises attacking with two forwards but can leave the midfield and defence exposed. Its advantages include boosting the attack with two forwards, increasing the chances of scoring, which is beneficial for teams with fast and effective forwards. However, it can leave a gap in the midfield, making transition and ball possession challenging, and requires a very strong and versatile midfielder.

1-2-3-1 System

In the 1-2-3-1 system, the team is organised with 1 goalkeeper, 2 defenders, 3 midfielders and 1 forward. This system focuses on controlling the midfield with moderate defensive support and a forward who can receive support from the midfielders. Its advantages include good midfield control and flexibility in attack, allowing for greater creativity and support from the midfield. However, it can be vulnerable to counter-attacks due to the fewer defenders and requires the defenders and midfielders to coordinate their positions well.

1-2-2-2 System

The 1-2-2-2 system arranges the team with 1 goalkeeper, 2 defenders, 2 midfielders and 2 forwards. This system balances defence, midfield and attack, providing options in all areas of the pitch. Its advantages include overall balance and versatility in play, allowing for quick transitions and good defence against the opponent's fast attacks. However, the effectiveness of this system depends on the coordination and communication between the lines and may lack dominance in the midfield if the midfielders are not strong enough.

Developing a Style of Play

The development of a team's style of play in cerebral palsy CP football is influenced significantly by the football culture of a country, the coach's tactical intentions, and the positioning of players according to their profiles, particularly their classification. These factors are in addition to the commonly accepted football-specific considerations.

It is essential to acknowledge that the varied physical, impairment and technical profiles of players in CP football, as well as modifications to the IFAB rules and Classification Rules implemented by the IFCPF, heavily impact the flow of the game.

Coaches must maintain a clear, undeterred vision aligned with their team's objectives when developing a style of play, recognising that this is still the sport of football. Having a well-defined game plan and ensuring players' ability to execute it are crucial for success both on and off the field. Thus, creating, developing and evaluating these objectives, using various points of reference such as the team's performance in training and competition, becomes a vital part of an ongoing process in developing a winning style of play. Table 7.1 provides examples of how changes to IFAB rules in CP football influence tactical decisions and the style of play.

Focusing on the core strengths of your player pool to develop a style of play requires consideration of the following (Table 7.2):

What Does Literature Say about CP Football Game Performance?

Previous research has focused on understanding the dynamics of CP football matches, with particular attention to technical and tactical performance indicators. For instance, Yanci (2015) conducted the first study analysing goals scored during 23 matches of the Spanish CP football championships. This study found that more goals are scored in CP football matches compared to mainstream football, particularly in the first half, during the first 15 minutes, and within the penalty area. Notably, most goals were scored when the ball was in play, with no goals scored from headers.[91]

More recent research has described methods of ball repossession, distribution and movement patterns that successfully led to goals in open play at the 2017 and 2018 Australian National CP football championships. This work highlighted that the majority of goals were scored in open play and in greater numbers than in mainstream football. The authors suggested that the most effective strategy for scoring goals in open play was passing the ball behind the last line of defence to a player who could either shoot or pass to a teammate to score.[94] Additionally, it was found that goals often resulted from sequences involving four or fewer passes before the shot.[94]

Table 7.1 Examples of the impact of the changes to IFAB rules in CP football in tactical decisions.

Rule	*Effect*
No offside	The game can be stretched, making it tactically challenging to squeeze teams between lines. It's common for a team to have at least one attacking player in their opponent's box when their own goalkeeper has the ball. In the final third attacking, players can stand on the goal line, making it difficult to leave them unmarked and therefore creating gaps across the field for the team to use on build-up. This leads to 1v1 or 1v0 match-ups throughout the flow of the game.
5 Substitutions	This rule allows a team, if they wish, to replace five of their six outfield positions (or goalkeeper) with 'fresh' players at any stage. This can impact the intensity of the game, creating a varied tactical challenge being presented by your opponent.
Classification	The IFCPF Classification system can significantly impact the style of play and tactical decisions. To ensure a fair game between two teams, each team has to have one FT1 player on the field at all times and is not allowed to have more than one FT3 player on the field. The rest of the team is made up of FT2 players. Notes: • FT1 ('most physically limited player'): If they play as a goalkeeper what does this mean on build-out and placement of other key players across the field? If the FT1 is an outfielder where and how can you deploy them effectively, matching their strengths to the positional role and ensuring the opponent doesn't exploit any weaknesses? • FT2 (mediumly physically affected): Where can these players be placed to cope with the opponent's strengths and weaknesses? • FT3 (most mobile player): Where on the field do you place your most mobile player while accounting for opportunities to minimise your opponent's strengths and exploit their weaknesses?

At the top-level competitions, Gamonales et al.[90] explored key performance determinants through notational analysis, focusing on sport class and player roles among other technical variables during the 2012 London Paralympic Games. The main results indicated that top-ranking teams and players with the highest functional profiles performed the most shots per match, predominantly using the central zones of the field. The right foot and instep were most commonly used for goal attempts, with low-height trajectories, although inside-foot kicks had the highest probability of scoring.[90] Similar findings

Table 7.2 Style of play considerations when creating a style of play according to the effects of CP football rules and classification.

Style of Play Consideration	*Key Questions*
Players' technical abilities	What are the technical attributes of your players, are they able or suited to complete the proposed game model?
Players' 'mentality'	Will the game model suit the player's social-physiological profile (defensive, attacking or patient mentality?)
Players' tactical understanding	Are the players able to comprehend and make real-time decisions based on the game model's expectations?
Football culture / expectations	What is the 'traditional' football style of play for the country? What are the intrinsic and extrinsic expectations of how a local or international team should 'look'?
Statistics of performance	Are you evolving your style of play based on facts? Does your team require this change based on self and opposition analysis? Is the style of play based on a particular rationale – what's the why of creating it?
Time available for development of style	Do you have enough time with the players to implement the style of play effectively?
Age and athleticism of players/team	Are your players mentally and physically ready for this change? Are they prepared to adapt to ensure the style of play is successful?
Classification	Do you have enough players of a particular IFCPF Classification available? Which positions do you have players in certain positions? Do injuries therefore mean a change in style of play?

were observed in a comparison of matches during the London 2012 and Rio 2016 Paralympic Games, with more shots at goal occurring in the last ten minutes of matches.[95]

Recently, Peña-González et al.[89] utilised video analysis to study goal patterns at the 2019 IFCPF World Cup, involving the top 16 national teams worldwide. They found that teams scoring first won the match 91.7% of the time. Top teams scored more and conceded fewer goals compared to bottom teams, with players with moderate impairments (i.e., FT2) scoring more goals than those in other classifications (i.e., FT1 and FT3), and a considerable prevalence of goalkeepers in the FT1 class (48.9%). Organised attacks were the most successful, accounting for 74.4% of goals, while counterattacks and set plays contributed to 18.1% and 7.5% of goals, respectively.[89]

Finally, while contextual factors influencing football performance are a well-explored topic in regular football,[92] limited studies exist in CP football. Henríquez et al.[69] compared the physical responses of footballers with CP using global positioning devices in matches played at sea level and moderate altitude. The study found that players exhibited lower activity profiles at moderate altitudes, with more pronounced effects during longer playing times. These findings indicate that contextual factors such as altitude exposure and match demands contribute to decreased physical responses, underscoring the need for tailored training and acclimatisation strategies.[69] Moreover, a novel study investigating contextual factors influencing match-physical performance of international-level CP footballers found that players from top-ranked teams covered more distance at low intensities compared to those from bottom-ranked teams. Matches against similar-level opposition required more physical effort in sprint distances and accelerations/decelerations for top-ranked teams, whereas bottom-ranked teams exhibited increased demands in total distance, running intensities and short-term actions. These results highlight the importance of considering contextual factors in training and support programmes for footballers with CP.

Conclusions and Practical Applications

Currently, there is a considerable volume of literature on CP football; however, substantial gaps remain to be addressed. Women's CP football, an emerging discipline experiencing rapid growth, requires further research to understand better the technical and tactical demands of the game due to its unique adaptations to the rules. Regarding the men's discipline, additional information is needed to comprehend tactical patterns and collective behaviour during competitions, where the use of global positioning technology can provide valuable data.[96]

This book chapter examines the technical, tactical and performance aspects of football for individuals with CP, highlighting the similarities and differences between mainstream football and CP football and emphasising the necessary adaptations. It describes technical characteristics such as the impact of different types of impairments on player abilities and strategies for optimising performance and discusses tactical considerations including player positioning and game strategies tailored to the unique requirements of CP football. Coaches and practitioners can use this information as a foundation for creating opportunities and training players with CP, fostering a dynamic and competitive sporting environment.

8 Physical Performance Assessment

Iván Peña-González, Juan Francisco Maggiolo, Jose Manuel Sarabia and Manuel Moya-Ramón

Contextual Framework

As reported by Yanci and colleagues in previous chapters and their scientific literature, a football player typically covers an average of 80–90 metres per minute and reaches peak speeds between 22 and 23 km/h. Additionally, a CP football player covers around 10–12 metres per minute at high intensity (>21 km/h) and between 3 and 4 metres per minute at sprint speed (>24 km/h), amounting to approximately 500 and 150 metres covered per match, respectively.[57, 76, 80] Furthermore, a CP football player performs more than 50 moderate to high-intensity accelerations and decelerations during a match, as well as more than 90 changes of direction at moderate to high intensity.[57, 76, 80] These data indicate that when assessing the physical performance of CP football players, it is essential to consider their ability to accelerate and reach high speeds in sprinting, their ability to change direction quickly and their capacity to cover long distances at high speeds with interspersed recovery periods.

Previous Approaches to Physical Performance Assessment in CP Football

The scientific literature on assessing physical performance in CP football is relatively new and initially emerged in association with the classification process. As previously observed in Chapter 5 of this book, evaluating players' functional capacity in typical actions of the sport is one of the objectives of the classification process. Therefore, much of the scientific literature on this topic has focused on finding valid, reliable and easily applicable physical assessment tests in the field, allowing classifiers to assess the impact of disability on the most common football actions that determine performance. The vast majority of tests used to assess physical performance in CP football are the same as those used in mainstream football, as seen in the previous section, because the physical requirements in competition are relatively similar, and any minor modifications are related to the distances covered due to the reduced dimensions of the playing field.

DOI: 10.4324/9781032708942-8

It may seem unusual that similar tests are used for assessing players' physical performance (as part of evaluating their sporting performance) and for assessing the impact of disability on the game (for classification purposes). However, as detailed before, the assessment of explosive actions is essential to understand a player's physical performance in competition. Likewise, these explosive actions (such as jumping, sprinting or changing direction rapidly) depend on muscular strength, require a high degree of speed in muscular contraction and demand high stability and coordination of movement. Given that the ability to produce force in a controlled manner, stability and coordination of movement are the primary impairments of individuals (and in this case athletes) with CP, it also seems evident that assessing these actions is indispensable for understanding the players' level of functionality in the game, as well as their performance.

While it is true that the early stages of research on assessing the physical performance of CP football players are associated with the classification process, overall, the scientific literature on this topic has proliferated in recent years (both for classification and sporting performance purposes). Although in practical terms, it was common to assess players' physical performance before there was much scientific literature on the subject, with the aim of evaluating players' fitness levels, designing and individualising training programmes and verifying the effectiveness of proposed training programmes. For these purposes, the most common physical tests in mainstream football have traditionally been used, applying the same protocols and assuming their validity and reliability in this population. This is relatively coherent, considering that the physical requirements in competition do not differ significantly between mainstream and adapted football. However, the scientific community has endeavoured to demonstrate the validity, reliability and usefulness of these tests in football players with CP.

Physical Performance Abilities Assessed in CP Football

Below are the physical qualities traditionally valued in football, along with the evidence supporting the use of these protocols in CP football:

Assessment of Jumping Ability

Jumping ability is a relevant quality in football, as it enables players to perform better in many game-related actions, such as heading a goal or contesting an aerial ball with an opponent. However, there are typically fewer jumping actions in CP football than in mainstream football, possibly due to the smaller dimensions of the field or impairments caused by disability. Nevertheless, jumping ability reflects athletes' capacity to generate high power, enabling them to exert force to overcome a given mass at the highest possible speed.

In an initial study in 2016, Yanci and colleagues[97] demonstrated the vertical jumping capacity of footballers with CP through tests such as Squat Jump (SJ) and Countermovement Jump (CMJ). They found that football players with CP jumped less than those without disability, and international CP football players jumped more than those competing nationally, providing these jumping tests with a certain discriminant validity.[97] Subsequently, in 2018, Reina and colleagues showed the validity and reliability of a group of jumping tests, both vertical and horizontal. Specifically, they demonstrated how the CMJ, as well as the horizontal jumping tests Standing Broad Jump, Four Bounds for Distance and Triple Hop, exhibited high criterion validity, high discriminant validity (by distinguishing between players of different sport classes) and high reliability values. These results indicate the feasibility of using both vertical and horizontal jumps to assess muscular performance (explosive strength/power) in CP football players.[71]

More recently, it has been found that the CMJ has become one of the most commonly used tests for assessing jumping ability in CP football players (Peña-González et al., 2021–22). However, at a practical level, this test may pose some challenges. Firstly, there is considerable variability in test execution among different CP profiles, which can affect jump technique and, consequently, its reliability. The CMJ assesses the utilisation of the elastic component, combined with the contractile capacity of the lower limb musculature, and requires keeping hands on the hips throughout the whole movement, which may be problematic for some profiles whose disability does not allow for this. For this reason, many studies using the CMJ to assess performance allow players to keep their hands free during the jump. This variant is sometimes referred to as the Abalakov test or CMJ-free, but this jump could be biased by the coordination ability of players. Additionally, highly asymmetric profiles (e.g., hemiplegic profile with unilateral spasticity) or those with coordination and stability issues (e.g., ataxic-athetotic profiles) will have very different jumping characteristics, which can influence the measurement.

Assessment of Sprint Speed

Traditionally, athletes' speed has been assessed by recording the time taken to cover a predetermined linear distance. While assessing maximum speed typically requires around 60 metres for sprint specialists, shorter sprint distances have been utilised in football to evaluate player speed. This adaptation is due to two main factors: first, football players, unlike sprinters, reach their maximum speed over shorter distances, and second, the distances covered during specific football actions are shorter. Specifically, in CP football, where field dimensions are smaller than in regular football, literature has investigated sprint speeds over distances ranging from 5 to 40 metres. It is widely accepted in the scientific community that sprint distances between 5 and 10 metres assess player acceleration capacity, whereas distances from 20 metres onwards indicate speeds relevant to the sport. Reina et al.[64] demonstrated how sprint speeds of international CP football players across various distances varied depending on sport class, providing discriminant validity to such tests. Studies by Peña-González et al.[32, 98–100] have further shown normative values for sprint tests across different distances among national and international CP football players, as well as variations in sprint performance based on sport class and training regimen.

On the other hand, the assessment of time (and thus speed) at different distances within the same sprint can indicate players' sprint profiles. In this regard, the evaluation of the sprint Force-Velocity (Fv) profile, as developed by Morin and Samozino, has emerged and been adapted to team sports in recent years. This sprint Fv profile estimates certain mechanical capabilities of athletes in sprinting. Consequently, it is possible to determine whether a player is more oriented towards horizontal force production in the first metres of the sprint (high acceleration profile) or towards movement speed. Specifically in CP football, it has been demonstrated that assessing the sprint Fv profile yields high reliability when performed with CP football players. Its validity is also evidenced, as it not only correlates with other physical performance assessment tests in CP football but also discriminates between players of different sport classes (FT1 < FT2 < FT3).[101]

The specific characteristics influencing sprint performance include the theoretical maximal capability of a player to produce horizontal force (F0) and velocity (V0), the associated maximal power output (Pmax), the theoretical maximal effectiveness of horizontal force application (RFmax), the player's capability to maintain the inevitable decrease in horizontal force production when velocity increases (DRF) and the maximal speed reached (Vmax).[102] With this information, coaches and conditioning trainers can analyse the specific components of players' sprint Fv profiles, which can be beneficial in determining players' strengths and weaknesses in sprint performance and in individualising their training programmes to enhance effectiveness and efficiency in player conditioning.

Assessing the Change of Direction Ability or Agility (With and Without Dribbling the Ball)

While we have delved into the importance of players' movement speed during competition, it is equally true that such high-intensity movements are often accompanied by rapid changes of direction. Although there is some controversy regarding the terms agility, pre-planned agility and change of direction, we currently understand the ability to quickly change direction during movement, in a planned manner and without responding to external stimuli, as 'Change of Direction Ability' (CODA). There are numerous tests that assess football players' ability to change direction rapidly. Among the most well-known are some that have been specifically used in CP football, such as the T-test and Illinois Agility Test (IAT).

Reina et al.[72] applied for the first time two of the most commonly used tests in regular football (the Modified Agility T-test [MAT] and the Illinois Agility Test [IAT]) in CP football. The MAT is a modification of the T-test, in which distances are halved (20 metres in total) and frontal, lateral and backward runs are performed, while the IAT is a test consisting of accelerations, changes of direction and slalom runs (always in a forward direction) during a circuit of approximately 60 metres. This study shows high reliability values for both tests, as well as demonstrating their validity for assessing CODA in this population. Subsequently, the validity and reliability of the MAT for assessing change of direction in international footballers with CP was also confirmed by Peña-González et al.[62] However, in the professional realm, the characteristics of the MAT, which requires lateral and backward movements and touching the cones with the hand during movements, led professionals and researchers to believe that a version of the MAT where movements were always frontal (in a forward direction) and the rule of touching the cone with the hand was eliminated could be more specific for football. In the work of Peña-González et al.,[32] a new protocol of the MAT with these characteristics is presented, which continues to exhibit very good validity and reliability values.

In the study by Reina et al.[64] mentioned earlier, in addition to the linear speed tests, it is demonstrated how the IAT discriminates between athletes with CP and the control group, as well as between some sport classes, although not all. Good reliability values for this test are also shown. As a key innovation, this study demonstrated the usefulness of conducting these tests both without the ball (CODA tests) and while dribbling (dribbling tests). In this regard, another factor that appears to be related to athletic performance and is present in the literature related to the conditioning assessment of CP football players is the ability to quickly change direction while dribbling the ball. Although ball dribbling is a technical skill, the ability to do so at higher speeds and while changing direction is closely linked to the player's physical capacity. In fact, dribbling ability can refer to a complex skill that reflects high performance in both technical and physical abilities.

Additionally, in the aforementioned study by Reina et al. [64] significant differences were shown between the same tests (linear sprint, Stop and Go test and IAT) performed with and without ball dribbling, indicating that these tests measure different theoretical constructs. Therefore, linear sprint (without the ball), CODA (without the ball) and dribbling (same tests but dribbling the ball) are distinct qualities to consider in CP football players. Furthermore, this work demonstrated how dribbling tests (the same tests but using the ball) better discriminated between players of different sport classes, although the reliability of these tests was reduced due to the use of the ball but still maintained acceptable values. Similarly, Daniel et al.[103] showed four examples of dribbling tests with good values of validity and reliability in CP footballers.

These tests are: (1) ball dribbling in a straight line, (2) ball dribbling with short slalom CODs, (3) ball dribbling with long slalom CODs and (4) ball dribbling in a square.[103]

More recently, in 2021, Yanci and colleagues investigated the use of the IAT and Stop and Go tests (with ball dribbling), as well as another dribbling test called the Turning and Dribbling test in a CP football sample. Although they showed acceptable reliability and validity values (differences between players with and without disabilities, as well as differences between players with different profiles of CP), no associations were found between these tests and the participants' competitive level, years of experience or degree of training.[65]

Peña-González and colleagues have demonstrated the use of the MAT for assessing both CODA (performing it without the ball) and dribbling (with the ball). To do so, they have developed a protocol to conduct both tests in a very similar manner.[32] Although there is currently no data in CP football regarding this new concept, dribbling ability could also be understood as the difference between a CODA test while dribbling the ball and the same CODA test without dribbling the ball.[104] This provides us with information on how much speed the player loses due to dribbling the ball, allowing us to identify different player profiles. These profiles range from those who are fast or slow in both the dribbling and non-dribbling tests to more technical profiles (little difference between with and without the ball) or more physical profiles (significant difference between the test with and without the ball). Future research should demonstrate the role of this concept of 'dribbling ability' in assessing the performance of CP football players.

Assessing Intermittent Endurance

CP football is a sport characterised by intermittent demands, where players primarily derive energy oxidatively through aerobic pathways. However, the decisive actions determining performance are highly rapid (explosive) and necessitate anaerobic energy production (utilising phosphagens and ATP synthesis via anaerobic glycolysis). Consequently, a CP football player's specific endurance must consider their ability to execute more high-intensity actions per minute and sustain a high level of efficiency in these intense actions throughout the match. This requires increased fatigue tolerance and enhanced recovery processes between intense actions for optimal sporting performance. Thus, assessing endurance in this sport necessitates intermittent protocols that evaluate the capacity to withstand high-intensity efforts over time with interspersed recoveries, mirroring the football profile.

In 2011, Kloyiam, Breen and Jakeman[105] utilised the Yo-Yo Intermittent Recovery Test (Level 1) (Yo-Yo IR1) to assess the specific endurance of a group of international CP football players. The Yo-Yo IR1 test is an intermittent endurance test in which players perform 40-metre sprints with a 180°

change of direction at the 20-metre mark. The test starts at a speed of 8 km/h and increases in speed with each block. To maintain the test's proposed speed, players must adjust their arrival at each mark to coincide with the auditory signal (beep) of the test. After each 40-metre run, players have a 10-second recovery before starting the next sprint. The test concludes when the player can no longer maintain the test speed and repeatedly fails to reach the 20- or 40-metre mark in time with the auditory signal. Upon test completion, the distance covered is assessed. In this and other studies, it has been demonstrated that international CP football players cover a significantly shorter distance during the test compared to able-bodied football players. However, likely due to the small sample size in these studies, no differences have been found between sports classes, although the player's position did affect the test outcome. The Yo-Yo IR1 has been widely used in CP football. The works of Peña-González and colleagues[98, 99, 101] have shown that (1) significant differences exist between classes in the distance covered in the test; (2) there is a correlation between Yo-Yo IR1 results and other performance tests in CP football; (3) performance in the test can be improved through a training process.

On the other hand, one of the most widely used and researched tests in regular football to assess intermittent endurance is the 30-15 Intermittent Fitness Test (IFT). In this test, fixed duration runs (30 seconds) with fixed rests (15 seconds) are conducted. With the work duration remaining constant, the athlete must cover increasing distances between auditory signals as the test speed increases, starting at 8 km/h and ending when the athlete can no longer maintain the speed. The test is performed over a 40-metre space, marked with three lines (at the ends and the centre). The auditory signals are designed to coincide with reaching each line according to the indicated speed. Finally, the test provides a velocity value called the final velocity of the IFT (vIFT). This value is of great importance not only for assessing the intermittent endurance of the player but also for subsequent exercise prescription, based on this value, which has been extensively studied in regular football. Although to date, no scientific references have been found regarding the use of the 30-15 IFT in CP football, several international teams are already integrating it into their assessment protocols. This is the case with the Spanish CP football team. Unpublished data has shown that the 30-15 IFT continues to maintain similar validity and reliability values to the Yo-Yo IR1, although it has advantages when programming endurance training based on test results.

Conclusions and Practical Applications

The following table (Table 8.1) presents a practical proposal for assessing the overall physical performance of CP football players. This proposal aims to evaluate the player comprehensively, based on scientific evidence, and by assessing the important physical requirements for CP football. Within

Table 8.1 Practical proposal for assessing the overall physical performance of CP football players.

Physical Performance Attribute	*Proposed Test*	*References in CP Football*	*Sample*	*Reference Values*
Jumping ability	Countermovement Jump (CMJ) – Free CMJ (without placing the hands at hips) [*Figure 8.1A*]	Yanci et al.[106]	International (n = 13)	CMJ = 24.33 ± 5.37 cm.
		Yanci et al.[97]	International (n = 12)	CMJ = 23.0 ± 5.4 cm.
		Reina et al.[71]	International (n = 132)	CMJ = 25.45 ± 6.1 cm.
		Coswig et al.[107]	Professional (n = 40)	CMJ = 27.8 ± 6.1 cm.
		Reina et al.[63]	International (n = 48)	CMJ = 44.0 ± 0.6 cm.
		Peña-González et al.[32]	National and international (n = 75)	CMJ = 16.18 to 23.64cm (FT1); 26.32 to 31.89cm (FT2); 25.54 to 46.06cm (FT3).
		Peña-González et al.[101]	International (n = 20)	CMJ = 24.58 ± 5.13cm (FT1); 34.19 ± 4.17cm (FT2); 35.30 ± 11.46cm (FT3); 31.64 ± 6.68cm (TOT).
		Peña-González et al.[100]	International (n = 15)	CMJ = 28.60 ± 6.18cm (pre); 32.79 ± 6.69cm (post).
		Peña-González et al.[99]	International (n = 14)	CMJ = 33.15 ± 7.21cm (pre); 32.99 ± 6.49cm (post).
Acceleration and linear velocity	Time at 5-m (in the 30-m linear sprint) [*Figure 8.1.B*]	Peña-González et al.[32]	National and international (n = 75)	5-m = 1.19 to 1.53s (FT1); 1.05 to 1.35s (FT2); 0.88 to 1.42s (FT3).
		Peña-González et al.[100]	International (n = 15)	5-m = 1.27 ± 0.15s (pre); 1.29 ± 0.14s (post).
		Peña-González et al.[98]	International (n = 15)	5-m = 1.28 ± 0.14s (pre); 1.18 ± 0.07s (post).
	Time at 30-m linear sprint [*Figure 8.1.B*]	Peña-González et al.[101]	International (n=20)	30-m = 5.71 ± 0.35s (FT1); 4.65 ± 0.20s (FT2); 4.65 ± 0.06s (FT3); 4.92 ± 0.52s (TOT).
		Peña-González et al.[99]	International (n = 14)	30-m= 5.08 ± 0.57s (pre); 4.92 ± 0.49s (post).
		Peña-González et al.[98]	International (n = 15)	30-m= 5.03 ± 0.53s (pre); 4.75 ± 0.29s (post).
Change of direction ability	Modified Agility Test (MAT) – Forward direction only [*Figure 8.1.C*]	Peña-González et al.[32]	National and international (n = 75)	MAT = 6.45 to 8.16s (FT1); 6.17 to 7.43s (FT2); 6.03 to 7.92s (FT3).
		Peña-González et al.[101]	International (n = 20)	MAT = 7.49 ± 0.41s (FT1); 6.14 ± 0.34s (FT2); 5.76 ± 0.13s (FT3); 6.44 ± 0.72s (TOT).
		Peña-González et al.[100]	International (n = 15)	MAT = 6.48 to 7.13s (pre); 6.17 to 7.09s (post).
		Peña-González et al.[99]	International (n = 14)	MAT = 6.74 ± 0.84s (pre); 6.46 ± 0.70 (post).
		Peña-González et al.[98]	International (n = 15)	MAT = 6.68 ± 0.77s (pre); 5.94 ± 0.30s (post).

(*Continued*)

Table 8.1 (Continued)

Physical Performance Attribute	*Proposed Test*	*References in CP Football*	*Sample*	*Reference Values*
Dribbling ability	Dribbling test with MAT structure [*Figure 8.1.D*]	Peña-González et al.[32]	National and international (n = 75)	Dribb = 10.69 to 15.52s (FT1); 8.09 to 13.61s (FT2); 7.53 to 13.72s (FT3).
		Peña-González et al.[101]	International (n = 20)	Dribb = 14.20 ± 4.52s (FT1); 9.40 ± 1.06s (FT2); 8.21 ± 0.53s (FT3); 10.48 ± 3.16s (TOT).
		Peña-González et al.[100]	International (n = 15)	Dribb = 10.91 ± 1.39s (pre); 11.01 ± 1.95s (post).
		Peña-González et al.[98]	International (n = 15)	Dribb = 11.34 ± 2.37s (pre); 8.95 ± 1.30s (post).
Intermittent endurance	Yo-Yo Intermittent Recovery 1 [*Figure 8.1.E*]	Kloyiam et al.[105]	International (n = 10)	Yo-YoIR1= 993 ± 397m.
		De Freitas et al.[87]	International (n = 11)	Yo-YoIR1= 516 ± 202m.
		Peña-González et al.[101]	International (n = 20)	Yo-YoIR1 = 344 ± 125m (FT1); 1074 ± 210m (FT2); 1540 ± 28m (FT3); 938 ± 418m (TOT).
		Peña-González et al.[99]	International (n = 14)	Yo-YoIR1 = 646 ± 267m (pre); 945 ± 425m (post).
		Peña-González et al.[98]	International (n = 15)	Yo-YoIR1 = 642 ± 2.44m (pre); 1145 ± 403m (post).

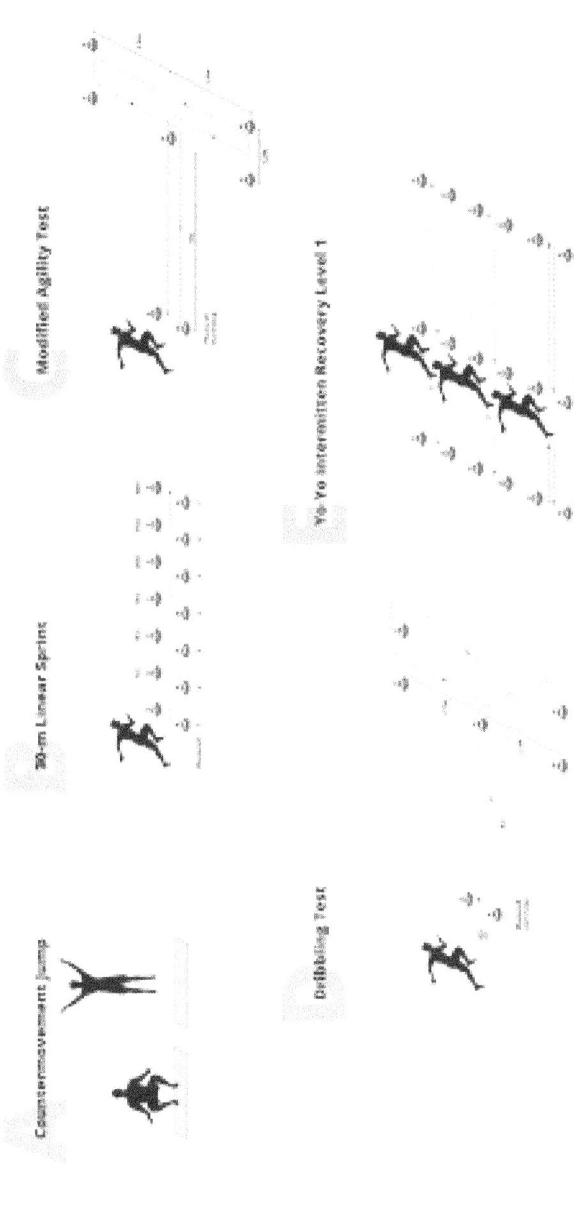

Figure 8.1 Graphical example of physical performance tests included in the practical proposal for assessing the overall physical performance of CP football players.

each physical requirement, the most useful tests have been selected, taking into account the scientific evidence provided in CP football, simplicity in application and time efficiency. Some of these tests have been shown by Peña-González et al.[32] to be effective in talent identification and selection of international players. Additionally, the table provides reference values, which may be useful for CP football coaches to compare. This proposal aims to provide coaches and physical trainers of CP football teams with a practical guide to the main field tests they can use for the conditional assessment of their athletes.

The physical performance assessment protocols encompass various essential aspects: sprint speed, change of direction ability (with and without dribbling the ball), jumping ability and intermittent endurance. Each test has been selected to reflect the specific demands of CP football, ensuring that assessments are both practical and scientifically valid.

By implementing these assessment protocols, coaches and physical trainers can systematically evaluate and enhance the performance of CP football players. This structured approach ensures that the unique physical demands of CP football are met, facilitating effective training programmes tailored to individual athlete needs. Overall, this proposal serves as a comprehensive guide for the conditional assessment of CP football players, promoting an evidence-based approach to optimise athletic performance and support talent identification and development within the sport.

9 Physical Conditioning for CP Footballers

Iván Peña-González, Juan Francisco Maggiolo, Alejandro Javaloyes and Manuel Moya-Ramón

Contextual Framework

Before delving into the physical conditioning of CP football players, it is essential to revisit some aspects covered in previous chapters of this book. Firstly, Chapters 1 and 5 explored how deficits in force production and control are among the primary impairments affecting individuals with CP. These impairments, along with challenges in movement coordination and stability, vary according to different CP profiles. Additionally, we have identified that the demands and requirements in CP football underscore the significance of actions dependent on muscular strength, performed at high speed (high intensity), and with considerable demands on movement control and stability, such as rapid changes of direction (Chapter 6). Given the importance of these actions, reliant on force production and muscular control and coordination, performance assessment tests often simulate typical football actions, such as jumps, sprints and changes of direction (Chapter 8).

Recommendations for the physical performance assessment of CP football players include jump tests, acceleration/speed tests, change of direction tests, dribbling tests and intermittent endurance assessment specific to football. Broadly speaking, these areas should be targeted for improvement to optimise the performance of CP football players in competition, as processes for assessing and developing athletic performance should be seamlessly synchronised and interlinked within sports planning.

All the previous information about the physical requirements in CP football, as well as the physical performance assessment, and the main limitations produced by the disability in developing the main actions of the game suggest that training programmes aimed at improving sports performance in CP football should focus on enhancing muscular strength (rapid force production or explosive strength). Additionally, these programmes should emphasise controlling movement and stability, along with the ability to repeat high-intensity actions intermittently, while maintaining the quality of those actions over time and delaying the onset of fatigue.

DOI: 10.4324/9781032708942-9

Are Athletes with Cerebral Palsy Able to Adapt to Physical Training?

The understanding of training protocols for athletes with CP, particularly in CP football, has markedly evolved in recent years. Previously, this domain was characterised by limited awareness. Reina et al.[72] demonstrated that international football players (representing ten national teams) engaged in an average of three football training sessions per week, complemented by three gym sessions. However, these findings exhibited considerable variance, with some athletes significantly exceeding or falling short of these averages. Furthermore, this information cannot be generalised to high-performance athletes at the national level, for whom there is a lack of data regarding the amount and type of training undertaken. At the national level, it is also common to observe a wide variety of training volumes and formats among players. Unofficial data from the Spanish Federation of Sports for People with CP (FEDPC) indicates that players licensed with this federation train between one and six days per week, incorporating a broad combination of training types. These range from football sessions (with CP football teams or mainstream teams) to strength/endurance training unrelated to football, and even to training in other sports disciplines or multi-sport training. This variation exists because there is no scientific evidence indicating which training formats are most effective for improving sports performance in CP football. Furthermore, Fleeton et al.[108] highlighted that, until recently, there was no scientific evidence that athletes with CP could adapt to training in a manner that improved their specific physical performance for their sports modalities.

Previous literature has explored how different training programmes impact physical fitness in the CP population.[109–111] Most of these approaches were based on strength training, as the impairment is related to muscle weakness due to alterations in structural and neurological muscle features.[108] This research has indicated the potential efficacy of muscle conditioning programmes in augmenting strength among this population. Such adaptations, similar to those observed in individuals without disabilities, include enhancements in muscle size (muscle hypertrophy) and improvements in muscle activation patterns (increased recruitment of muscle fibres or reduced co-contraction). This foundational evidence underscores the adaptability of individuals with CP to structured training interventions. Furthermore, specific training stimuli have been shown to yield distinct adaptations, as documented by Moreau et al.[112] highlighting variances in responses to strength-based versus speed-based training paradigms. Such beneficial effects, which may include increased muscular strength, alteration of muscle pennation angles or improvement of neurological control, are of paramount importance in CP football players due to the actions that determine performance, as well as the primary limitations faced by players due to their disability.

However, despite the promising implications of strength training interventions for individuals with CP, several challenges persist. Many studies in this realm focus on paediatric populations or sedentary individuals with CP, limiting the generalisability of findings to athletic cohorts. These studies often included sedentary populations, children and/or individuals with a high level of impairment (levels II–III of the GMFCS), whereas CP football players are characterised by a low activity limitation (level I of the GMFCS). Additionally, diverse methodologies employed across studies, including variations in intervention duration, exercise modalities and intensity levels, impede direct comparisons of adaptation outcomes. Training programmes used in previous literature are heterogeneous, often focused on therapies, and not tailored to a low-impaired or highly trained CP population (such as CP footballers). Finally, while improvements in strength have been demonstrated, the translation of these gains into tangible performance enhancements remains uncertain. Attempts to assess 'performance' parameters have often relied on metrics associated with quality of life or daily functionality in sedentary individuals or children (such as walking tests), potentially misrepresenting the challenges faced by athletic populations, particularly in CP football.[108]

Physical Performance Adaptations to Specific Conditioning Training in CP Football

Having demonstrated the capacity of individuals with CP to adapt to muscular training, the challenge lies in applying a performance-focused approach to the training of athletes with CP. This approach emphasises multi-joint exercises performed at high intensity/velocity and places emphasis on high-demand task assessment, aiming to optimise sport-specific adaptations and facilitate meaningful transfer in function and performance within this population.

Alarcón et al.[113] proposed a type of eccentric strength training performed on a 'Leg Press' machine, three days per week for six weeks. This programme consisted of four sets of eight repetitions at 80% of the one-repetition maximum (1RM), focusing on the eccentric part of the execution. This study demonstrated improvements ranging from 1.5% to 15.4% in maximal isometric knee extensor muscle strength, in strength asymmetry between legs and in thigh perimeter. Additionally, they achieved more sport-specific adaptations such as improved balance as assessed by the Y-balance test. However, the ability to change direction in a specific field test (more closely linked to specific performance in football) was not altered following the training programme.

In 2020, during the COVID-19 mandatory lockdown period, Peña-González et al.[100] conducted an online training programme with international CP football players. The programme spanned 12 weeks, divided into two blocks of six weeks each, as outdoor training was permitted halfway through the programme. The training regimen consisted of four weekly sessions, with two sessions focused on strength improvement (days one and three) and two sessions aimed at enhancing endurance (days two and four) (Table 9.1). This was the first study to demonstrate the effects of a regular training programme on the physical performance of international CP football players. The primary objective was to maintain the physical performance of international CP football players during the COVID-19 lockdown period. The results showed that this 12-week training programme, consisting of four weekly sessions focused on maintaining strength and endurance during the lockdown, contributed to maintaining (or even improving) football-specific physical fitness (jump, acceleration, sprint velocity, change of direction and dribbling) even without specific football training sessions.

Also in 2020, Umar et al.[114] demonstrated a training programme consisting of 24 sessions, conducted three days per week over eight weeks. This programme involved circuit training comprising eight stations, each with a different focus (strength, balance, coordination, speed of movement, agility, change of direction, and endurance). However, no further details are provided regarding the specific exercises used or the specific volumes and intensities of each exercise. The authors reported improvements in speed (sprint) and change of direction (20% to 50% improvement) in 14 international CP football players.

In 2023, Peña-González et al.[99] showed significant moderate to high improvements in international CP football players' physical performance (sprint, change of direction and intermittent endurance) after a 25-week training programme. This programme comprised two football-specific training sessions per week plus two additional strength training sessions. The specific objective of the strength sessions was to improve force application for acceleration and displacement velocity. The programme included six strength exercises (squat, frontal lunge, side lateral lunge, hip thrust, deadlift and ankle plantar flexion) performed at low intensity (body weight) due to their limited experience in strength training but executed at maximum possible velocity during the concentric phase. The training load was progressively increased, primarily through an increase in volume (sets and repetitions):

Weeks 1 to 5: 3 sets of 8 repetitions (24 repetitions per exercise).
Weeks 6 to 10: 3 sets of 10 repetitions (30 repetitions per exercise).
Weeks 11 to 15: 3 sets of 12 repetitions (36 repetitions per exercise).
Weeks 16 to 20: 4 sets of 10 repetitions (40 repetitions per exercise).
Weeks 21 to 25: 4 sets of 12 repetitions (48 repetitions per exercise).

This work confirmed the adaptability of footballers with CP to sports training and demonstrated the specificity of adaptations depending on the training focus. Analysis of the sprint F-v profile (discussed in the previous chapter) showed an improvement in the F0 variable (maximum theoretical ability to apply force in the horizontal vector in the initial metres of a sprint), while actual and theoretical maximum velocity remained unchanged after the training

Table 9.1 Description of the self-training programme by Peña-Gonzalez et al.[100]

Period 1 (weeks 1 to 6)						
Day 1		Day 2	Day 3		Day 4	
6 exercises	Day off	*1 circuit*	*6 exercises*	Day off	*1 circuit*	Day off
4 bouts/exercise		*4 rounds/ circuit*	*4 bouts/exercise*		*4 rounds/ circuit*	
12 rep/bout		*6 exercises/round*	*12 rep/bout*		*6 exercises/round*	
30 s. rest/bout		*30 s. work–30 s. rest*	*30 s. rest/bout*		*30 s. work–30 s. rest*	
1 min rest/exercise		*1 min. rest/round*	*1 min. rest/exercise*		*1 min. rest/round*	
Squat		Low skipping	Squat		Low skipping	
Lunge		Lateral-sided jumps	Lunge		Lateral-sided jumps	
Side lateral lunge		Repeated jumps	Side lateral lunge		Repeated jumps	
Hip thrust		High skipping	Hip thrust		High skipping	
Deadlift		Triple hop	Deadlift		Triple hop	
Ankle plantar flexion		Burpees	Ankle plantar flexion		Burpees	
Period 2 (weeks 7 to 12)						
Day 1		Day 2	Day 3		Day 4	
6 exercises	Day off	*4 bouts × 4min.*	*1 circuit*	Day off	*2 blocks × 6 bouts × 30 s. all out running*	Day off
4 bouts/exercise		*high intensity running*	*4 rounds/circuit*		*30 s. rest/bout*	
12 rep/bout		*(> 80% FCmax)*	*6 exercises/round*		*2 min. rest/block*	
30 s. rest/bout		*3 min. rest/bout*	*30 s. work–30 s. rest*			
1 min rest/exercise			*1 min. rest/round*			
Squat			Low skipping			
Lunge			Lateral-sided jumps			
Side lateral lunge			Repeated jumps			
Hip thrust			High skipping			
Deadlift			Triple hop			
Ankle plantar flexion			Burpees			

programme. This study showed improvements in specific football actions, such as reduced time in a 30-metre sprint, primarily attributed to improved acceleration capacity through greater force application, as maximum achieved velocity remained unchanged. There were also improvements in change of direction actions (MAT), attributed to increased braking and re-acceleration capacity (dependent on strength), and improvements in an intermittent endurance test linked to enhanced force application during acceleration, as this test (Yo-Yo IR1) involves continuous accelerations, decelerations and changes of direction in its protocol.

In this regard, a connection between strength training (combined with regular football training) and adaptations related to sprinting, acceleration and change of direction appears to be demonstrated, an aspect already widely demonstrated in athletes and footballers without disabilities. Strength training methods are associated with improvements in sprinting, attributed to increased lower body strength. Enhanced overall strength contributes to greater force production, which is essential for people with CP. Individuals with CP, particularly those with less severe impairments, can derive similar benefits from strength training as non-disabled athletes, leading to improvements in sport-specific physical performance, including sprinting.

Long-Term Physical Performance Development

Based on the foregoing information, coaches could design long-term training programmes, considering the potential adaptations that different types of training may have on the physical performance of football players with CP. As discussed in Chapter 3, the main international sporting events in CP football are the World Championships, held every two years, and the continental championships, also held biennially. The work of Peña-González and Moya-Ramón[98] presented a training progression used in preparation for the IFCPF World Cup 2022, detailing the four phases or training cycles undertaken by a national CP football team. During this preparation period, which lasted over a year, various assessments of physical performance were conducted after the completion of each training phase or cycle. Table 9.2 shows the specific training programmes followed during each phase of the preparatory period.

The long-term training programme presented by Peña-González and Moya-Ramón demonstrated significant improvements in acceleration and sprinting, ranging from 5% to 11% throughout the preparatory period. Additionally, it showed improvements of 11% for change of direction, 21% for dribbling and 78% for players' intermittent endurance, all of which were significant. These results indicate that football players with CP are capable of adapting to sports training, with improvements specific to the orientation of the training applied.[98]

The inclusion of strength training, ranging from bodyweight exercises to resistance training sessions, impacts the improvement of players' applied

Table 9.2 Description of the four training periods of the programme developed by Peña-González and Moya-Ramón.[98]

Training Period	*Number and Type of Sessions*	*Training Characteristics*
1	2 Strength training sessions	*Volume*: 4 × 15s/12rep (circuit) *Intensity*: Own weight *Exercises*: Frontal plank; Crunches; Hip thrust; Squat; Front lunge (R); Front lunge (L); Hip adduction; Push ups
2	2 Strength training sessions	*Volume*: 4 × 12rep *Intensity*: Own weight *Exercises*: Squat; Front lunge (R); Front lunge (L); Hip thrust; Ankle plantar flex (R); Ankle plantar flex (L)
	1 Long-HIIT session	*Volume*: 4 × 4min (3min rest: walking) *Intensity*: 70% vYIR1 *Exercise*: Running
	Circuit after sessions (2 times per week)	*Volume*: 4 × 15s (circuit) *Intensity*: Own weight *Exercises*: Frontal plank; Lat plank (R); Lat plank (L); Back plank; Crunch; Push-ups
3	2 Strength training sessions	*Volume*: 4 × 12rep *Intensity*: Own weight *Exercises*: Squat; Front lunge (R); Front lunge (L); Hip thrust; Ankle plantar flex (R); Ankle plantar flex (L)
	1 Long-HIIT session	*Volume*: 10 × 2min (1min rest: walking) *Intensity*: 80% vYIR1 *Exercise*: Running
	Circuit after sessions (2 times per week)	*Volume*: 4 × 15s (circuit) *Intensity*: Own weight *Exercises*: Frontal plank; Lat plank (R); Lat plank (L); Back plank; Crunch; Push-ups
4	2 Strength training sessions	*Volume*: 4 × 30s:15s (work:rest) (circuit) *Intensity*: Own weight *Exercises*: Front lunge (R); Front lunge (L); Side lunge (R); Side lunge (L); CMJs; High skip; Ski lateral jumps; Jumping jacks
	1 Resistance training session	*Volume*: 3 × 10rep *Intensity*: 10(15) *Exercises*: Squat; Leg-ext; Leg-curl; Ankle plantar flex; Press bench; Lat pulldown; Shoulder press
	1 Long-HIIT session	*Volume*: 2 × 10 × 1min (30s rest: walking/2min rest) *Intensity*: 90% vYIR1 *Exercise*: Running
	1 Short-HIIT session	*Volume*: 2 × 8 x 30s (15s rest: walking) *Intensity*: 100% vYIR1 *Exercise*: Running
	Circuit after sessions (2 times per week)	*Volume*: 4 × 15s (circuit) *Intensity*: Own weight *Exercises*: Frontal plank; Lat plank (R); Lat plank (L); Back plank; Crunch; Push-ups

strength in sport-specific tasks such as acceleration and change of direction. Research has shown that strength training, particularly eccentric strength training, can significantly enhance muscle strength and balance. Additionally, incorporating strength training exercises, such as squats, lunges, hip thrusts and deadlifts, performed with progressive overload, has been shown to improve the force application necessary for acceleration and sprinting in CP football players.

Furthermore, the inclusion of specific high-intensity interval training (HIIT) during this training programme provided new and relevant information about the potential for improvement in this quality among international CP football players. Studies during the COVID-19 pandemic[100,114] have demonstrated the effectiveness of HIIT in improving endurance, speed and change of direction. As shown in these works, progressively incorporating HIIT training sessions in a running format, combining short and long HIIT formats, can be a highly effective way to greatly enhance football-specific endurance.

A well-structured, long-term training programme, incorporating both strength training and HIIT, can lead to significant improvements in the physical performance of CP football players. This programme should be tailored to the specific needs and abilities of the athletes, ensuring a balance between various types of training to optimise overall performance and achieve sport-specific goals.

Conclusions and Practical Applications

Given the primary physical limitations resulting from CP, most training programmes designed for individuals with this disability have been strength-based, focusing primarily on rehabilitation and physical performance enhancement. However, these programmes may not be fully applicable to CP football, as they have often been developed for populations with a high degree of disability, sedentary individuals or paediatric populations. Furthermore, many of these programmes have had a rehabilitative focus, and the measurement instruments and protocols used may not be suitable for athletes with a moderate-to-high level of training.

Recent literature on CP footballers has shown that these athletes can achieve training adaptations similar to those of individuals without disabilities, provided the training stimuli and orientations are appropriately tailored. Systematic training programmes for international CP football players have demonstrated that specific physical performance can be developed and assessed using field tests over the medium and long term. Training programmes for football players with CP should consider various factors, including the starting performance level and training experience of the athletes. More specifically, the type of CP (reviewed in Chapter 1) should inform specific adaptations to each exercise or task. For example, a lower body strength exercise might be designed as a bilateral and guided task for a player with coordination-balance issues, while a unilateral task with more degrees of freedom might be more suitable for a player with spastic hemiparesis. These adaptations rely on the professional experience of coaches and the individualisation of tasks for specific cases encountered in practical settings. However, studies have not consistently shown differences in training adaptations among players of different sport classes (FT1, FT2 or FT3). This may be due to the small sample sizes in studies, which do not allow for statistical comparison between groups. Currently, there is no evidence to suggest significant differences in the ability to adapt to training among FT1, FT2 and FT3 players, beyond possible differences related to their initial performance states at the beginning of the training programme. In general, it appears that including 2–3 strength sessions per week, combined with regular football training, improves not only strength but also specific football tasks such as jumping, acceleration and changes of direction. These improvements result from specific adaptations that may be structural or neurological, depending on the applied stimuli. However, the specific stimuli most effective for maximising these improvements have not yet been thoroughly investigated.

Endurance training based on high-intensity interval training (HIIT) methods has been shown to improve the ability to repeat intermittent running efforts, as demonstrated in numerous studies on non-disabled athletes, including footballers. There is no reason to believe that the physiological and mechanical improvements observed in regular sports cannot also occur in athletes with CP in a similar manner. Nonetheless, CP football involves many factors that can influence high performance, and the isolated training of different physical qualities without integrating technical and tactical factors specific to football may pose a challenge in training these factors efficiently. Therefore, integrated methodologies, such as training based on small-sided games (SSG), are gaining popularity in regular football and have shown performance improvements similar to those of isolated training methods. However, there is still no substantial evidence on the effectiveness of improving specific physical performance through 'played' or 'integrated' tasks in CP football. Future research should focus on exploring these integrated methodologies to determine their potential benefits for CP football players.

10 CP Football Team Management

Eduardo Cervelló, Tomás García-Calvo and Francisco Leo

Contextual Framework

The study of CP football team management is deeply rooted in a comprehensive contextual framework that synthesises theoretical and practical insights into team dynamics, leadership and motivation. This chapter delves into the scientific basis of how coaches' behaviours, and group processes influence players' actions and overall team performance. Central to this framework is the quality of coach–athlete relationships, which significantly impacts group cohesion, goal development, communication and role responsibilities within the team. These relationships are often analysed using models such as the 4Cs (Closeness, Commitment, Complementarity and Co-orientation), which highlight the emotional, cognitive and behavioural dimensions of the coach–athlete dyad. Leadership models such as the Multidimensional Model of Leadership and the Transformational Leadership Model elucidate how different leadership styles and behaviours affect team dynamics, player satisfaction and performance. These models, which include authoritarian, democratic and laissez-faire styles, as well as transformational and transactional leadership approaches, provide a robust framework for understanding the complex interactions between coaches and players.

Additionally, the motivational climate established by coaches, as explained by Self-Determination Theory and the TARGET framework (Task, Authority, Recognition, Grouping, Evaluation, Time), plays a crucial role in shaping athletes' engagement, motivation and performance. A task-involving climate that promotes learning and mastery, as opposed to an ego-involving climate that emphasises competition, fosters better individual and collective motivation. Team cohesion, divided into task and social cohesion, is essential for maintaining unity and achieving goals. This cohesion is influenced by positive coaching behaviours like instructional leadership, feedback, democratic behaviours and social support, while minimising autocratic behaviours.

Furthermore, collective efficacy, the group's shared belief in its capability to succeed, is enhanced by strong coach–athlete relationships and effective leadership, leading to improved team performance, resilience and higher satisfaction

DOI: 10.4324/9781032708942-10

levels. Research has shown that perceptions of coach leadership and positive coach–athlete relationships positively influence collective efficacy, resulting in greater team resilience and higher performance levels. This integrated framework not only guides scientific inquiry but also provides practical recommendations for optimising team management and performance in CP football. By focusing on these interconnected elements, coaches can adopt strategies that significantly improve the functioning and success of sports teams. This holistic approach ensures that both individual players and the team as a whole can achieve their highest potential, thereby enhancing both individual and collective outcomes in the highly competitive environment of CP football.

Identifying Processes Related to Coach Behaviours

Scientific research has identified several processes crucial for enhancing sports performance and player well-being. This section will present key aspects, specifically tailored to CP football.

Quality of the Coach–Athlete Relationship

Research indicates that fostering optimal interactions between coach and athlete significantly impacts group processes such as cohesion, goal development, communication and role definition within the team.[115, 116] Jowett proposes the 4Cs model as a framework for studying the interdependence in coach–athlete relationships; encompassing feelings, thoughts and behaviours; and evaluating the rapport in these dimensions.

Closeness

This factor involves the emotional bonds between coach and athlete, including respect, trust and mutual appreciation.

Commitment

This factor relates to the intentions and thoughts regarding maintaining a long-term relationship.

Complementarity

This reflects the behaviours of coaches and athletes aimed at achieving performance goals. It includes reciprocal behaviours initiated by the coach and accepted by the athlete, and concordant behaviours where both parties engage in effective communication and openness to suggestions.

Co-orientation

This marks the extent to which the coach and athlete's feelings, thoughts and behaviours are in sync, reflecting a shared understanding of their partnership.

Studies have linked the quality of the coach–athlete relationship with effective leadership, cohesion and collective efficacy. For instance, Vella et al.[117] demonstrated that leadership processes and collective efficacy are influenced by the interpersonal dynamics between coach and athlete. Additionally, social cohesion is correlated with the player's perceived closeness and commitment to their coach.[118]

Leadership Models in CP Football

Coach Leadership

Leadership in sports is an interactive process where the leader guides and influences the team towards common goals.[119] Several models analyse leadership within the sporting context:

Multidimensional Model of Leadership[120]: This model posits that team performance and player satisfaction depend on the alignment of the coach's behaviours with the players' preferences in specific situations. Coach behaviours are classified as authoritarian, democratic or laissez-faire.

Transformational Leadership Model[121]: This model integrates three types of leadership – transformational, transactional and laissez-faire. Transformational leadership involves influencing and connecting with the group, transactional leadership involves a dependent relationship where the coach provides necessary resources, and laissez-faire is characterised by passive leadership.

Player Leadership

Recent research emphasises the significance of players' roles in team leadership processes.[122] Player leadership can be defined as an athlete who influences team members towards a common goal. Leadership roles within a team include:

Task Leader: Provides tactical advice and adjustments.
Motivational Leader: Encourages optimal performance.
Social Leader: Promotes a positive team atmosphere off the field.
External Leader: Manages communication with management, media and sponsors.

High-quality athlete leadership is associated with increased team efficiency, resilience and performance.[123]

Motivational Climate Generated by the Coach

The perception of the motivational climate created by the coach significantly impacts athletes' behaviour. A climate emphasising norm-based evaluation and competition promotes ego involvement.[124] Conversely, a climate focusing on skill mastery and effort fosters task involvement. Coaches influence motivational climates through training design and the information provided before and during competitions.

From the perspective of self-determination theory,[125] coaches who support player autonomy fulfil the needs for competence, autonomy and social relationships, resulting in higher levels of autonomous motivation. In contrast, controlling coaching styles elicit more controlled forms of motivation. Autonomous motivation involves intrinsic motives and values alignment, while controlled motivation is driven by external rewards and obligations.

By understanding these processes, coaches can better support CP football players, enhancing their performance and overall well-being.

Identifying Processes Related to Group Behaviours

Team Cohesion

The term group cohesion, as defined by Carron et al.[126] refers to the dynamic emergent state 'reflected in the tendency of a group to stick together and remain united in the pursuit of its instrumental goals and/or for the satisfaction of the affective needs of its members' (p. 213). Carron and colleagues developed a conceptual model to explain group cohesion perceptions. This model suggests that each team member can develop two types of perceptions: one related to the group as a unit, called group integration, which pertains to each athlete's perception of similarity, proximity, bonding and unity within the group; and another related to personal satisfaction and goals, called individual attraction to the group, reflecting each athlete's individual motivations for remaining in the group. Furthermore, they indicated that perceptions of cohesion could be related to task cohesion, reflecting the degree to which group members work together to achieve common goals, or to social cohesion, reflecting the degree to which team members empathise with each other and enjoy the group's camaraderie. Thus, four manifestations of team cohesion are identified: task integration into the group (GI-T), social integration into the group (GI-S), individual attraction to the task group (ATG-T) and individual attraction to the social group (ATG-S).

Research has demonstrated that coach behaviours significantly impact cohesion levels. For instance, players who perceive their coaches as demonstrating training and instructional leadership, positive feedback, democratic behaviour, social support and low levels of autocratic behaviour generally exhibit higher levels of social and task cohesion within the team.[127]

Additionally, teams led by coaches perceived as competent and fair by their players show higher levels of cohesion.[128, 129]

Collective Efficacy

Bandura[130] described collective efficacy as 'the group's beliefs about its capability to organise and execute the courses of action required to achieve specific accomplishments' (p. 476). These beliefs are generally influenced by factors such as group size, group cohesion, athletes' previous experiences, leadership and the motivational climate within the team. Based on these factors, a group perception of the team's collective efficacy is formed, leading to various cognitive, affective and behavioural outcomes.

Research has linked coach behaviours to the collective efficacy of the group and its evolution throughout a season.[131] Studies show that perceptions of coach leadership and coach–athlete relationships positively influence perceptions of collective efficacy.[132] Moreover, Leo et al.[127] demonstrated that perceptions of positive leadership behaviours, such as training instruction, perceived social support, positive feedback and democratic behaviours among team members, are stronger predictors of collective efficacy than perceptions of autocratic leadership by coaches.

This section has outlined some of the most accepted theoretical models in the scientific community that explain effective team leadership, as well as the most relevant research contributions. Below, we propose a series of practical recommendations to enhance leadership effectiveness in CP football teams.

Consequences and Practical Implications

In this section, we present a series of practical recommendations that are not exclusive to any single theoretical model but should be understood as a comprehensive approach to team leadership in CP football.

Strategies Focused on Coach Behaviours

Within the team structure, various strategies can be employed to enhance the coach–athlete relationship, improve leadership qualities, foster player leadership and enhance the motivational climate within the team. Here, we will discuss strategies related to these aspects, aimed at improving team structure processes.

Coach–Player Relationship

Jowett and Shanmugam[133] have proposed several strategies to improve the quality of relationships between coach and player. To develop closeness, one should: be trustworthy with confidences, remain loyal, avoid entertaining criticisms and gossip among athletes, maintain neutrality in conflicts between athletes, keep promises, be open to suggestions, create an innovative and creative environment, be honest, focus on the person rather than just the athlete and express feelings genuinely. For commitment, actions such as developing individualised programmes, establishing goal-setting programmes, involving the athlete in the training process and decision-making, ensuring the athlete is responsible for the goals set and committing the necessary time to achieve them are essential. Lastly, complementarity can be enhanced by coordinating training actions with the athlete, setting an example, creating communication channels (e.g., regular meetings, tutoring), developing competence, organising well-planned training structures and instilling hard work as a performance guide.

Leadership

Analysing the main theories and their evolution to date, it appears that more flexible leadership methods are associated with positive outcomes. Therefore, giving greater prominence to followers (athletes) in decision-making, persuading athletes, fostering a positive work climate, displaying authentic behaviours and considering athletes' opinions and needs can generate transformational and authentic leadership in coaches. Additionally, sharing leadership with players is crucial. This can be achieved by identifying team leaders, training them to exercise leadership (including increasing the number of captains), clarifying expectations, defining the specific functions of each leader (task leader, social leader, external leader and motivational leader) and informing them on how to improve their leadership roles within the team.

Motivational Climate

The TARGET framework is the most widely used for creating task-involving motivational climates. Thus, the way Task (T) is designed as a challenge, the Authority (A) source providing choice options, the Nature of Recognition (R) given privately and based on individual progress, the Grouping (G) method fostering peer interaction, the Evaluation (E) based on task mastery and individual improvement and the Time (T) offered to execute tasks tailored to each athlete are crucial for generating a task-involving motivational climate. Additionally, from the perspective of self-determination theory, creating an autonomy-supportive interpersonal style by the coach fosters an appropriate climate. This can be achieved by offering choices to athletes, allowing them freedom in certain decision-making, understanding their interests and motivations, using non-controlling language and providing meaningful information about the behaviours required for self-management.

Strategies Focused on Group Behaviours

This section presents practical applications aimed at fostering group cohesion and collective efficacy, centred on promoting unity, cooperation and trust within the team.

Group Cohesion

Athletes spend a significant amount of time in their sporting environment due to training, travel and camps. Therefore, it is important that they feel integrated into the group. Different dynamics can be proposed to improve task and social cohesion: promoting acquaintance among teammates; integrating new players by coaches and leaders, explaining their roles and expectations; enhancing team identification through chants, pre-competitive routines, mottos, clothing, music, mascots, etc.; cooperative tasks to increase interactions within the group; defining players' roles and functions on the field; establishing team goals agreed upon with the players; and organising extracurricular activities.

Collective Efficacy

Trust in the abilities of each player and the team is crucial for competition. Coaches can undertake various strategies to involve their players in their development. To increase levels of collective efficacy among players, we can refer to past team achievements to reinforce players positively, foster peer leadership, provide reinforcing feedback in training and competitive matches, stimulate a task-oriented motivational climate during training sessions, reduce intra-team conflicts, promote unity, facilitate information exchange, develop mutual trust in the team's capabilities, establish clear team expectations, create challenging training tasks tailored to players' skill levels and use videos of past team performances demonstrating desired achievements.

By implementing these strategies, coaches can enhance the overall effectiveness and cohesion of CP football teams, leading to improved performance and player well-being.

Conclusions and Practical Applications

This book has elucidated various theoretical models and practical strategies essential for enhancing the performance and well-being of athletes in CP football. Understanding the dynamics of group cohesion, collective efficacy, coach–athlete relationships and motivational climates is paramount for fostering a successful team environment.

Group cohesion is critical, as highlighted by Carron et al.'s conceptual model, which underscores the importance of both task and social cohesion within the team. Effective strategies to enhance cohesion include promoting acquaintance among teammates, integrating new players, clearly defining roles and expectations, and organising team-building activities. Collective efficacy, based on Bandura's theory, emphasises the significance of a shared belief in the team's capabilities. Practical applications to boost collective efficacy involve reinforcing past achievements, fostering leadership among peers, providing constructive feedback and creating a task-oriented motivational climate. The coach–athlete relationship is another vital component. According to Jowett and Shanmugam, strategies to improve this relationship focus on developing closeness, commitment and complementarity. Coaches should build trust, involve athletes in decision-making and maintain open communication channels. Effective leadership in CP football requires a flexible approach that gives prominence to athletes' input and promotes transformational and authentic leadership styles. Sharing leadership responsibilities with players, particularly through identifying and training team leaders, is also crucial for team success. Finally, the motivational climate plays a significant role. The TARGET framework and self-determination theory provide valuable guidelines for creating a supportive and task-involving motivational climate. Coaches should design challenging tasks, provide autonomy and use non-controlling language to foster intrinsic motivation among athletes.

To enhance team cohesion, it is important to organise acquaintance activities that allow teammates to get to know each other better, fostering a sense of unity and belonging. Coaches and team leaders should actively help new members understand their roles and feel welcomed, and use symbols, chants and routines to strengthen team identity and pride. Boosting collective efficacy can be achieved by highlighting and celebrating past successes to build confidence in team capabilities. Training players in leadership roles enhances peer support and team cohesion, while maintaining regular, positive communication and feedback loops reinforces collective goals. Strengthening coach–athlete relationships requires trust-building actions that demonstrate reliability and honesty. Inclusive decision-making involves athletes in setting goals and planning training sessions, and consistent communication through regular meetings and feedback sessions ensures alignment and mutual understanding. Implementing effective leadership involves adapting leadership approaches based on team needs and individual athlete preferences. Shared leadership, where team leaders are identified and empowered, distributes leadership responsibilities and enhances team dynamics. Creating a positive motivational climate involves designing challenging yet attainable training sessions that promote skill development and engagement. Providing athletes with choices and involving them in decision-making processes fosters autonomy support, while using supportive and informative language encourages self-motivation and personal growth. By integrating these insights and applications, coaches can significantly enhance the effectiveness and cohesion of CP football teams. The practical strategies outlined in this book offer a comprehensive framework for fostering a positive, supportive and high-performing team environment, ultimately leading to improved athletic performance and player satisfaction.

11 Differential Medical and Health-Related Issues

Daniel Bueno

Contextual Framework

CP is a disorder resulting from a non-progressive injury to a developing brain, characterised by abnormal tone, posture and movement.[134] Despite the term 'Cerebral Palsy Football', CP is not the only medical diagnosis encompassed within the sport, as seen in previous chapters of this book. Individuals with traumatic brain injury, stroke, multiple sclerosis or post-surgical brain sequelae are also eligible to participate. This diversity in diagnoses implies that players may have varying medical risks and health-related issues. The first part of this chapter will present some of the most common medical conditions associated with these diagnoses.

Medical Risk and Management

Epilepsy

Epilepsy is a disorder characterised by the tendency for unprovoked seizures.[135] The prevalence of epilepsy varies according to the medical diagnosis of the players. Between 10 and 60% of individuals with CP have epilepsy, with the wide range explained by the correlation between the severity of CP and the prevalence of epilepsy.[136] Despite this frequent association with severity, epilepsy prevalence as high as 24–50% has been reported in individuals with mild CP (GMFCS I-II), who are the primary participants in CP football. Among the types of CP, epilepsy is more frequent in individuals with spastic hemiplegia than in those with spastic diplegia.

Furthermore, individuals with MS have a higher risk of epilepsy, although the prevalence is not higher than 2%.[137] Similarly, epilepsy post-stroke in young people is common, with prevalences between 6 and 11% in some series.[138]

The pharmacological management of epilepsy extends beyond the scope of this chapter, but it is crucial to note that most antiepileptic drugs are not included in the World Anti-Doping Agency (WADA) prohibited list for 2024. These drugs include valproic acid, carbamazepine, lamotrigine and

DOI: 10.4324/9781032708942-11

levetiracetam, among others. However, athletes are responsible for verifying their medication against the current prohibited list. A common adverse effect of antiepileptic drugs is drowsiness; however, there is no evidence to suggest this impacts football performance.[139]

Epilepsy often induces fear among athletes, families and technical staff regarding the practice of contact sports. Given that CP football can involve collisions or heading the ball, some misunderstandings can arise. Epilepsy, in itself, is not a contraindication for playing football; a thorough risk assessment is necessary. The main concern in sports practice for individuals with epilepsy is the risk of injury during a seizure episode. This risk is comparable to that present in daily activities such as crossing the street or climbing stairs. Some sports, like climbing, motor sports and water sports, are categorised as high-risk if a seizure occurs.[140] Team sports like football are considered low-risk in terms of seizure-related injuries.[140] Moreover, the risk of seizure exacerbation due to football practice is low, and physical activity can contribute to better seizure control.[141] In conclusion, athletes who adhere to their medication and have good control of their condition can participate in CP football with no significantly higher risk than athletes without epilepsy. Coaches, medical staff and athletes must understand that proper field management aims to minimise injuries due to sudden loss of consciousness.

Respiratory Symptoms

Although respiratory comorbidities are usually associated with severe CP, there are reports of a high prevalence of respiratory symptoms in individuals with mild CP.[142] Up to 33.9% of individuals with mild CP report a weekly cough, and around 12% report weekly wheezing.[142] While these reports focus on the paediatric population, a history of recurrent wheezing during infancy is a significant risk factor for exercise-induced bronchoconstriction (EIB).[143] EIB is characterised by transient bronchoconstriction due to exercise, with spontaneous recovery post-exercise. It can be triggered by cold air and environmental irritants and is known to impair athletic performance.[143]

In addition to EIB, some authors have reported lower respiratory pressure and function in individuals with mild and moderate CP compared to those without CP.[144] Although these authors suggest a neuromuscular compromise of respiratory muscles and impaired chest mobility, the lack of standardisation of CP severity and fitness levels makes these results hard to interpret for CP football. Nevertheless, due to the intermittent aerobic and anaerobic efforts in open areas during football practices, CP players may be at increased risk of EIB.[143] It is advisable to be vigilant for symptoms of wheezing, chest tightness or coughing during or after exercise (e.g., in the dressing room). If available, spirometry to rule out asthma can be a valuable addition to pre-participation screening.

For diagnosing EIB, eucapnic voluntary hyperpnoea is the gold standard test, though it is not easily accessible in all areas. An exercise-induced test can be useful. The test involves an aerobic challenge without a warm-up, rapidly increasing intensity to 80–90% of maximum effort, with spirometry performed before and at various intervals after the test. More information on performing the test can be found in other resources.[143]

Management of EIB includes non-pharmacological and pharmacological strategies. High volumes of cold air during ventilation are a trigger for EIB, so a gradual aerobic warm-up with increasing intensity is recommended. Adequate fluid intake is also crucial to prevent airway dryness. Pharmacological treatments include inhaled corticosteroids (ICS) and long-acting beta-2 agonists (LABA). While ICS use is not considered doping under the 2024 WADA guidelines, some types and doses of LABA are. Therefore, checking the prohibited list regarding LABA types and doses is recommended to make the best choice.

Hip Displacement

Hip displacement is a common condition in individuals with CP during infancy, typically due to muscle tone and strength imbalances.[145] It is more frequent in individuals with more severe motor impairment and is associated with hip pain and future hip osteoarthritis (OA).[146] However, individuals with mild CP can also have asymptomatic hip displacement.[145] There are no studies describing the risk of asymptomatic hip conditions in CP and their impact on sports participation. However, while evidence is emerging, it could be prudent to review risk factors for other hip conditions.

Although hip development dysplasia has a different pathophysiology, acetabular dysplasia and abnormal proximal femoral geometry are identified alterations in CP hips.[146] Athletes with hip development dysplasia may be at higher risk of femoroacetabular impingement (FAI).[147] There is no evidence linking hip displacement in CP with FAI risk, but it is possible that FAI could develop in some CP athletes due to bone and joint abnormalities.

In the absence of evidence to form accurate guidelines, it is suggested to review the clinical history of hip displacement to document musculoskeletal injuries in these athletes as evidence emerges. Although most CP football athletes do not have hip displacement, recognising anatomical and morphological risk factors for hip pain in athletes is useful to identify those at higher risk.[148] Known risk factors for hip displacement include greater impairment, leg length discrepancy, hip adduction issues and hemiplegic gait (Winters IV gait classification).[149] Considering these factors during pre-participation evaluation and documenting them in the medical history could be sufficient.

Given that hip pain is associated with multiple risk factors, a multi-component exercise training programme that includes assessment, mobility, strengthening of hip and trunk muscles, multi-planar training and load monitoring could help reduce the risk of developing hip pain during practice.[148]

Ankle Contractures

Individuals with CP, even with very mild motor impairment, can have ankle contractures due to imbalances in muscle tone and strength. The calf muscles are key in the hypertonia MIC. Consequently, some degree of ankle contractures will be common among CP football participants, often seen as lack of heel touch or excessive knee hyperextension during walking. In terms of running and sprinting, lack of dorsiflexion during the flight phase could impact the vertical force applied at ground contact, making it difficult to achieve an active push-off.[150] This could compromise the speed that the athlete generates, or the strategy used for sprinting. For example, subjects with spastic CP often increase step cadence rather than step length to increase speed, have increased hip range of motion (ROM) instead of ankle or knee ROM for sprinting and generate less power in the knee and ankle compared to individuals without CP.[151]

Lack of ankle dorsiflexion, such as seen in CP individuals with ankle contractures, could be a risk factor for injuries during sprinting due to restriction of subtalar joint movement and compensatory strategies.[152] Proper load management, full ROM strengthening and continuous ROM improvement with training are good strategies. The use of stretching exercises, although evidence is conflicting, can be beneficial. Passive stretching exercises have not shown significant value in treating contractures in children with CP.[153] However, in non-CP subjects, passive stretching protocols have shown to increase ROM, but to a similar extent as strength exercises.[154] In the author's experience, the low internal and external load exerted by passive stretching compared to some strengthening variants allows for high-frequency inclusion with fair to good results as a complement to strength and sport-specific practice.

Botulinum toxin A (BONT-A) can be considered for treating severe spasticity in the calf. BONT-A has shown good results in treating ankle contractures when used with a serial casting protocol.[153] However, this approach has some issues. The use of botulinum toxin must be reported as a new treatment due to its potential impact on impairment and athlete classification. Additionally, BONT-A can affect muscle force, potentially impacting the push-off phase of sprinting. Serial casting, although effective, can cause transient muscle atrophy, impairing athletic performance for several weeks post-treatment.

Surgical treatments, such as Achilles tendon enlargement, should also be considered. Many players have undergone previous surgical procedures when starting CP football. These procedures can affect spasticity evaluation and muscle strength.[155] If muscle contracture management is indicated for health reasons such as pain, it must be reported to the International Federation of

Cerebral Palsy Football and consider changes in motor performance and physical conditioning needs.

Physiotherapy, Recovery and Injury Prevention

Injury Risk

The injury risk among athletes is a crucial aspect to address. During the Rio 2016 Paralympic Games, pre-competition and competition injury rates were documented for various sports, with CP football being one of the sports with the highest injury incidence rates.[156] Similarly, the surveillance data from the London 2012 Paralympic Games indicated that most injuries during the games were acute, with only 7% being overuse injuries.[157] Additionally, it has been reported that the ankle and knee are the most common injury sites, and CP athletes predominantly suffer from soft tissue injuries throughout their athletic careers.[158] However, despite extensive injury surveillance efforts, the data remains limited. For instance, only 14 documented injuries were recorded during the London 2012 Games, encompassing a heterogeneous group in terms of CP severity, which limits the generalisability of these findings.[159]

Several risk factors for injury in football have been identified, including previous injuries, genetics, shoe-surface interaction, load and neuromuscular factors such as asymmetries and biomechanics.[160] Most injuries occur in the ankle, knee, groin and thigh, with two-thirds being traumatic and primarily occurring in the initial or final 15 minutes of the match.[160] This data highlights the importance of warm-up and fatigue management in injury prevention. Considering that CP players are more prone to fatigue, have coordination difficulties and face challenges during deceleration and CODA, these factors could increase the risk of collisions or contact injuries.

Ankle Sprains

Ankle sprains are prevalent, particularly affecting the collateral ankle complex, most commonly the anterior talo-fibular ligament due to inversion sprains.[161] Weakness in the ankle evertor muscles is a known risk factor for ankle sprains, which is a common issue among CP players.[162] Therefore, preventive strategies such as proprioceptive training are recommended.[163] However, due to neurological impairments, the effectiveness of balance, proprioceptive and peroneus strengthening exercises may quickly plateau in some players. This limitation makes external aids like bracing or taping attractive options. Bracing or taping has been shown to play a role in preventing ankle sprains, particularly in individuals with previous sprains, without significantly impacting performance.[164] Bracing, in particular, has a better number needed to treat compared to taping, especially in those without prior injuries. Therefore, it is recommended to use ankle bracing for players at higher risk of ankle sprains.

Muscle Injuries

Hamstring strains are the most common non-contact injury in football, typically occurring during sprinting.[165] Progressive sprint exposure may reduce the risk of hamstring injuries, although evidence regarding sprinting biomechanics as a risk factor in able-bodied individuals is conflicting.[165] For CP athletes, altered sprinting biomechanics and asymmetries lack robust evidence as risk factors for injury. Clinically, it is challenging to analyse how different profiles of athletes, regarding spasticity, muscle contractures, impaired muscle power and coordination, can affect hamstring injury risk. Questions such as whether a weak hamstring overloads the non-impaired side or itself due to high velocity achieved with the non-impaired leg remain unanswered. Given that biomechanical factors are not clear even in able-bodied individuals, it is unlikely these questions will be resolved soon. Therefore, similar principles for hamstring injury prevention should be applied, with progressive exposure to sprinting actions, monitoring the volume of exposure to acceleration and maximal velocity phases.

Physiotherapy for CP Athletes

The principles of physiotherapy for CP athletes align with those for individuals without CP, with some additional considerations.

Cold/Cryotherapy

The use of cold therapy has been debated due to potential performance impairment or delayed recovery from injuries. However, there is no high-quality evidence suggesting significant delays in recovery or soft tissue healing. Given its effect on pain reduction, judicious use of local cold therapy to control excessive inflammation and pain is warranted. For CP athletes, the transient spasticity impairment caused by cold should not deter its use.

Heat Therapy

Heat therapy, including hot compresses, follows the same guidelines as for individuals without CP. It is primarily used for musculoskeletal pain and can have beneficial effects on spasticity in CP athletes.[166]

Non-invasive Electrotherapy

Superficial electrotherapy, such as transcutaneous electrical nerve stimulation (TENS), is widely used for pain management.[167] Intensity is usually guided by patient tolerance, and caution is needed for individuals with sensory impairments, such as those with TBI or post-stroke. Electrical muscle stimulation

(EMS) is beneficial for muscle weakness, particularly in cases where progressive overload is challenging.[168]

Dry Needling

This invasive physiotherapy technique, used to alleviate muscle pain, has shown short-term effects on spasticity in stroke patients.[169]

Invasive Electrotherapy

Techniques such as ultrasound-guided neuromodulation and percutaneous electrolysis have gained popularity. These involve the use of sterile needles and currents to promote recovery, particularly in tendon injuries. Detailed descriptions of these interventions are available in specialised resources.

Muscle Strengthening

Strength training does not impair spasticity in CP or post-stroke subjects and is beneficial for muscle strength, jumping, sprinting and CODA. Although there are no specific guidelines for rehabilitation after muscle injuries in CP athletes, the principles are similar to those for individuals without CP. The plasticity of CP muscles allows them to respond to training stimuli, making strength training an essential component of physiotherapy. Techniques such as blood flow restriction, though not widely studied for rehabilitation purposes, have shown safe use for performance in CP athletes.[170]

Conclusions and Practical Applications

This study underscores the importance of understanding the unique characteristics and health risks associated with athletes participating in CP football, which includes a range of diagnoses beyond cerebral palsy, such as traumatic brain injury, stroke and multiple sclerosis. These conditions present varied medical risks and health-related issues that must be meticulously addressed by technical and sports medicine teams.

Epilepsy, with its significant prevalence among CP athletes, necessitates careful management, especially given the anxiety associated with contact sports. Despite the inherent risks, appropriate treatment and compliance enable athletes to participate without significant additional danger. Respiratory symptoms, including exercise-induced bronchoconstriction, require vigilant monitoring and the potential use of pre-participation spirometry to ensure athlete safety and performance.

Hip displacement and ankle contractures, common in CP due to muscle tone imbalances, demand thorough medical history reviews and customised physiotherapy to manage pain and prevent injuries. The high incidence of injuries in CP football underscores the need for effective preventive training and injury management strategies, including proper load monitoring, proprioceptive training and potentially bracing for high-risk individuals.

Cryotherapy, while debated, remains a valuable tool for pain management in soft tissue injuries, with its transient effect on spasticity not posing significant limitations. These findings highlight the critical role of a multidisciplinary approach in optimising the health and performance of CP football athletes, suggesting that thorough pre-participation assessments and individualised treatment plans are essential for mitigating risks and enhancing athletic outcomes.

12 Differential Features of Female CP Football

Matías Henríquez, María Isabel Cornejo and Heather Jameson

Contextual Framework

Women's football has undergone continuous development and increasing popularity worldwide, as evidenced by the 13.36 million girls and women who practise and compete at various levels.[171] This growth has been supported by an expanding number of competitive opportunities and training facilities, enhancing the professionalism and expertise required to advance high-performance standards.[172] Over the past decade, as women's football has become more professional, there has been a surge in research dedicated to understanding and improving performance in this domain, now comprising approximately 20% of all football-related research.[173]

This successful movement has also influenced football modalities for individuals with disabilities, particularly for players with CP, whose participation is widespread and offers opportunities to men and women with impairments such as spastic hypertonia, ataxia or dyskinesia (athetosis/dystonia).[58] Notably, the women's modality is gaining popularity, alongside the growing number of participants and international competitions available for this para-sport.

The first internationally sanctioned competition under the IFCPF was the World Cup held in May 2022 in Salou, Spain. In 2023, significant milestones were achieved with the first regional competitions, followed by the eagerly anticipated second edition of the World Cup in 2024. In the following section, the distinct features of women's CP football will be described, introducing this population and exploring the characteristics of the game.

Adaptations to Rules for Women's CP Football

As previously discussed in the section on game rules (Chapter 4), women's CP football adheres to the regulations set by the IFAB, with specific adaptations to accommodate players with physical disabilities. To reiterate, the women's modality follows the same rules as the men's counterpart regarding the classification of participants, allowing the inclusion of players who meet

DOI: 10.4324/9781032708942-12

the minimum criteria for the three eligible impairments (i.e., spastic hypertonia, ataxia or dyskinesia).[60] Furthermore, the same classification structure is applied in competition, permitting a maximum of one FT3 player (e.g., minimal impact of impairment) and requiring at least one FT1 player (e.g., severe impact of impairment) to be on the field throughout the game.[12]

A notable distinction from the men's counterpart is that the women's modality is played with five players per side, features shorter match durations (e.g., two halves of 25 minutes) and takes place on a smaller field (e.g., 40 x 27 metres).[174] Other rules remain similar to those in the men's modality. This summary serves as a reminder of the specific characteristics and requirements of women's CP football.

Women Footballers with CP

Before delving into the abilities and capacities of women footballers with CP, it is important to highlight key aspects of female participation in parasport. In recent years, there has been a growing emphasis on the development of women's sports worldwide. However, when analysing the landscape for individuals with disabilities, particularly girls and women, data indicates that this demographic is more likely to experience disability compared to men.[175] Additionally, numerous studies have explored the health advantages of sports participation, such as improved cardiovascular health, mental well-being and overall quality of life.[176] Despite these benefits, research has revealed that women tend to be less physically active than men.[177] These factors highlight the 'double discrimination' that women with disabilities often face in society, making it even more challenging for them to practise and access sports.

In this context, Ascondo et al.[178] have studied the barriers and facilitators for women in sports and found that women perceive more barriers than men, with the most significant being intrinsic or personal in nature. Moreover, there is the issue of the 'invisibility' or poor media coverage of female athletes and the scarcity of female athletes who are global leaders in sports contexts.

To gain a comprehensive understanding of this topic, it is crucial to explore the historical development and inclusion of women in sports. Initially, the Olympic Games, established in 1894, primarily aimed to showcase the athletic prowess of men, excluding women until the Paris Games in 1900. This marked the first instance of women being allowed to compete, engaging in sports such as golf and tennis, where Charlotte Cooper became the first woman to win an Olympic medal in an individual event. The Paralympic movement originated after the Second World War from the Stoke Mandeville Games, which held its first international competition for athletes with disabilities in 1952. The first official Paralympic Games for men and women athletes were held after the Summer Olympic Games in Rome in 1960.[36] While women with disabilities had the opportunity to participate in the Paralympic

Games, the gap in the number of events by gender was evident, particularly in 1988 when female participation was only 22%. Since then, women's participation has increased steadily, reaching approximately 42% at the Tokyo 2020 Paralympic Games.

Various strategies have been proposed to promote women's participation in Paralympic sports. Some team disciplines have suggested the inclusion of women in 'mixed-gender' or 'sex-integrated' events, where men and women compete together. These events have been promoted by the International Paralympic Committee (IPC) as a means to achieve gender parity. However, Dean et al.[179] have shown that this approach might not be the most effective for promoting women's participation, as mixed-gender events often perpetuate stereotypical gender imbalances and can further marginalise or discourage women from participating. They emphasise that these sports offer little opportunity for women to engage with the broader Paralympic movement.

In light of these points, the IFCPF proposed the development of the sport with all-women teams. However, this initiative did not materialise until 2022, when the first Women's World Cup took place in Spain, featuring the participation of five countries (the USA, Australia, The Netherlands, Japan and Spain). Despite being held concurrently with the men's World Cup, which somewhat overshadowed the women's event, this tournament marked a significant milestone. It led to a review and update of the game rules and qualification criteria to address the specific needs of women's CP football.

It is hoped that women's CP football will continue to grow globally, providing valuable opportunities for women and girls with hypertonia, ataxia or dyskinesia to engage in sports.

Sex Differences in the Physical Capacity of Footballers with CP

Previous studies have reported sex differences in multiple physical capacities of regular footballers, which are necessary to meet the demands of the game. These capacities include running capacity, sprint ability, change of direction, jump capabilities, technical components and match performance characteristics, among other factors. However, there is limited information regarding sex differences in the physical capacities of individuals with CP. Previous reports analysing the aerobic and anaerobic capacity of children with CP described differences between participants with typical development and found no differences according to sex among participants with similar profiles (i.e., male children with CP vs. female children with CP).[180] Furthermore, a systematic review found controversial results, suggesting an overrepresentation of male children with CP and limited evidence of sex differences in neuromotor outcomes in most of the studies analysed.[181] Recently, Henríquez et al.[58] reported lower sprint and change of direction performance in women compared to

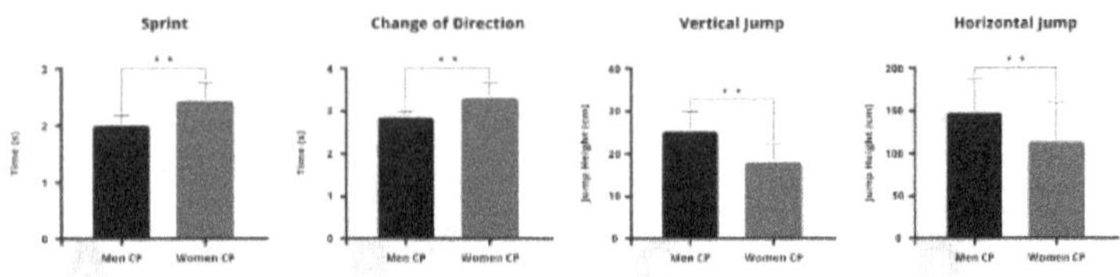

Figure 12.1 Preliminary results from an unpublished work of Cornejo, comparing the physical performance in sprint, CODA and jump between men and women.

men footballers with CP, providing novel information to better understand this population and develop individualised training programmes. Preliminary results of an unpublished work by Cornejo (Figure 12.1), analysing the performance of male and female footballers with CP in sprinting, CODA and jumping capacity suggest significant differences and lower performance in the female group.

General Characteristics of Women Footballers with CP

Understanding the physical, technical and tactical characteristics of women footballers with CP is essential for individualising training and optimising the diverse abilities of the players. Currently, there is limited information about the physical profile and game demands of women in CP football, and unpublished data can provide a preliminary insight into this group. During the 2022 IFCPF Women's World Cup, five national teams from four continents competed, and the players underwent various physical tests as part of the classification process. Forty-five players performed tests to assess change of direction using the 505 test, vertical jump using the countermovement jump, horizontal jump using the standing broad jump and football skills using the dribbling speed test. The main results (unpublished) showed that, on average, the participants completed the 505 test in approximately 3.3 seconds, the dribbling speed test in approximately 19.8 seconds, achieved a vertical jump height of approximately 17.7 cm and a horizontal jump distance of approximately 121.0 cm.

Regarding physical performance during competition matches, an unpublished study found that women players with CP can cover a total distance of approximately 67.0 metres per minute, reach a maximum speed of approximately 17.0 km/h, and achieve maximum acceleration and deceleration rates of approximately 4.7 m/s^2 and -5.6 m/s^2, respectively. The physical demands during matches for women's CP football are likely different from those of

Figure 12.2 Graphical representation of most commonly used playing systems in female CP football.

their male counterparts, particularly considering the lower number of players (e.g., 5-a-side) and the reduced field size.[182] This aspect warrants further investigation, especially considering the different sports classes, to elucidate the particular demands of this discipline.

Like mainstream football, the women's modality employs tactical strategies adapted to the rules and characteristics of the players. Coaches can use various tactical schemas suitable for the 5-a-side game, such as the 1-2-1-1, 1-3-1 and 1-1-2-1 formations.

Despite the limited information available about training monitoring and performance in women footballers with CP (see Figure 12.3), existing literature on mainstream football can provide some foundational principles for working with this population. A recent narrative review by Beato et al.[183] suggests that practitioners should include both objective and subjective methods to monitor performance and readiness in training for women footballers.

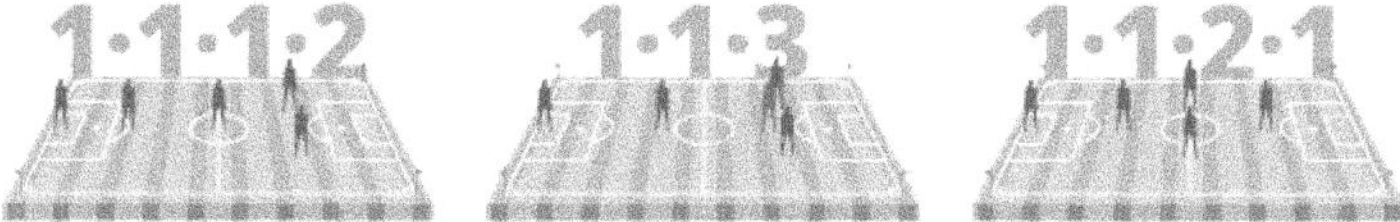

Figure 12.3 Picture of two female CP football players competing in an international championship match. Photo courtesy of the IFCPF.

The use of countermovement jumps and subjective perceptual scales that incorporate menstrual cycle-related questions could be useful for measuring readiness, in addition to nutritional strategies aimed at optimising iron metabolism.[183] It is important to note that these suggestions consider the significant interindividual variation in impairment profiles and the different abilities of players according to their field positions.

Conclusions and Practical Applications

The rising popularity of women's CP football and the expansion of competitive opportunities have led to increased interest in understanding and improving performance in this sport. As more research focuses on women's football, there is a growing need to address the intersection between adaptations in rules, performance and training methods to accommodate players with physical disabilities, such as those participating in women's CP football. Preliminary findings suggest that women footballers with CP may have lower sprint, change of direction and jumping capacities compared to their male counterparts; therefore, more research is needed to describe these sex differences comprehensively.

To optimise performance and training for women footballers with CP, coaches can tailor tactical strategies to suit the 5-a-side format of the game, taking into account the physical characteristics of women players with CP. While there is still limited information on training monitoring and performance in women footballers with CP, insights from mainstream football can provide a foundation for developing effective strategies.

References

1. Leonardi, M., et al. (2022). 20 Years of ICF - International Classification of Functioning, Disability and Health: uses and applications around the world. *Int J Environ Res Public Health*, 19(18).
2. Tweedy, S. M., & Vanlandewijck, Y. C. (2011). International Paralympic Committee position stand-background and scientific principles of classification in Paralympic sport. *Br J Sports Med*, 45(4).
3. Rosenbaum, P., et al. (2006). A report: the definition and classification of cerebral palsy. *Dev Med Child Neurol*, 49(6).
4. Vitrikas, K., et al. (2020). Cerebral palsy: An overview. *Am Fam Physician*, 101(4).
5. Jones, M. W., et al. (2007). Cerebral palsy: Introduction and diagnosis (Part I). *J Pediatr Health Care*, 21(3).
6. Morgan, P., et al. (2018). Cerebral palsy. In Dulac, O., Lassonde, M. & Sarnat, H. B. (Eds.) *Handbook of clinical neurology*. Elsevier.
7. Zollman, F. S. (Ed.). (2021). *Manual of traumatic brain injury*. Springer.
8. Murphy, S. J., & Werring, D. J. (2023). Stroke: causes and clinical features. *Medicine*, 51(9).
9. Cook, A., & Giunti, P. (2017). Friedreich's ataxia: clinical features, pathogenesis and management. *Br Med Bull*, 124(1).
10. Mondal, B., et al. (2013). An update on Spino-cerebellar ataxias. *Ann Indian Acad Neurol*, 16(3).
11. Cans, C., et al. (2007). Recommendations from the SCPE collaborative group for defining and classifying cerebral palsy. *Dev Med Child Neurol*, 109.
12. IFCPF. (2018). *Classification rules and regulations*. International Federation of Cerebral Palsy Football.
13. Rethlefsen, S. A., et al. (2010). Classification systems in cerebral palsy. *Orthop Clin North Am*, 41(4).
14. Sanger, T. D., et al. (2003). Hypertonia in childhood. *Pediatrics*, 111(1).
15. Graham, H. K., et al. (2016). Cerebral palsy. *Nat Rev Dis Primers*, 2(1).
16. Roldan, A., et al, (2021). To what degree does limb spasticity affect motor performance in para-footballers with cerebral palsy? *Front Physiol*, 12.
17. Sanger, T. D., et al. (2010). Definition and classification of hyperkinetic movements in childhood. *Mov Disord*, 25(11).
18. Ashizawa, T., & Xia, G. (2016). Ataxia. *Continuum*, 22.
19. Zhang, Q., et al. (2021). Clinical recognition of sensory ataxia and cerebellar ataxia. *Front Hum Neurosci*, 15.

20. Hogarth, L., et al. (2019). Classifying motor coordination impairment in Para swimmers with brain injury. *J Sci Med Sport*, 22(5).
21. Ogoke, C. C. (2018). Clinical classification of cerebral palsy. In Al-Zwaini, I. J. (Ed.) *Cerebral palsy – clinical and therapeutic aspects*. IntechOpen.
22. Palisano, R. J., et al. (2008). Content validity of the expanded and revised Gross Motor Function Classification System. *Dev Med Child Neurol*, 50(10).
23. Burns, F., et al. (2014). The cerebral palsy transition clinic: administrative chore, clinical responsibility, or opportunity for audit and clinical research? *J Child Orthop*, 8(3).
24. World Health Organization. (2001). International classification of functioning disability and health. WHO.
25. de Hollander, E. L., & Proper, K. I. (2018). Physical activity levels of adults with various physical disabilities. *Prev Med Rep*, 10.
26. Lai, B., et al. (2021). Leisure-time physical activity interventions for children and adults with cerebral palsy: a scoping review. *Dev Med Child Neurol*, 63(2).
27. Wely, L., et al. (2014). The effectiveness of a physical activity stimulation programme for children with cerebral palsy on social participation, self-perception and quality of life: A randomized controlled trial. *Clin Rehabil*, 28.
28. Groff, D., et al. (2006). Effects of a therapeutic recreation intervention using exercise: a case study with a child with cerebral palsy. *Ther Rec J*, 40.
29. Graham, H. K., et al. (2016). Cerebral palsy. *Nat Rev Dis Primers*, 2.
30. Thomason, P. (2020). Functional mobility and gait in children and youth with cerebral palsy. In Miller, F. Bachrach, S. Lennon, N. O'Neil, M. E. (Eds.) *Cerebral palsy*. Springer
31. Fowler, E. G., et al. (2007). Promotion of physical fitness and prevention of secondary conditions for children with cerebral palsy: section on pediatrics research summit proceedings. *Phys Ther*, 87.
32. Peña-González, I., et al. (2021). Physical performance differences between Spanish selected and nonselected para-footballers with cerebral palsy for the national team. *Int J Sports Physiol Perform*, 16(11).
33. Blauwet, C. A., & Willick, S. E. (2012). The paralympic movement: using sports to promote health, disability rights, and social integration for athletes with disabilities. *PM&R*, 4(11).
34. Tweedy, S. M. (2002). Biomechanical consequences of impairment: a taxonomical approach. *Adapt Phys Act Q*, 19(1).
35. Hutzler, Y. (2003). Physical activity and sports for people with disabilities: future directions and trends. *Sport Sci Rev*, 12(1–2), 49–88.
36. DePauw, K. P., & Gavron, S. J. (2005). *Disability sport*. Human Kinetics.
37. Brittain, I. (2010). *The paralympic games explained*. Routledge.
38. Bailey, S. (2008). *Athlete first: a history of the Paralympic movement*. Wiley.
39. International Paralympic Committee, IPC. (2015). *IPC announces final Tokyo 2020 Paralympic sports programme*. IPC.
40. Bundesliga. (n.d.). All you need to know about soccer. https://www.bundesliga.com/en/faq/all-you-need-to-know-about-soccer
41. FIFA. (2023). *FIFA releases Global Women's Football Landscape Survey Report*. Fédération Internationale de Football Association.
42. The International Football Association Board. (n.d.). The IFAB background.
43. The International Football Association Board. (2023a). *Laws of the game*. IFAB.

44. The International Football Association Board. (2023b). *Notes and modifications*. IFAB.
45. IFCPF. (2023). *Classification rules and regulations*. International Federation of CP Football.
46. IFCPF. (n.d.). *History of CP football*. International Federation of CP Football.
47. Nieuwenhuijsen, C., et al. (2011). Physical fitness, everyday physical activity, and fatigue in ambulatory adults with bilateral spastic cerebral palsy. *Scand J Med Sci Sports*, 21(4).
48. Beckman, E. M., & Tweedy, S. M. (2009). Towards evidence-based classification in Paralympic athletics: evaluating the validity of activity limitation tests for use in classification of Paralympic running events. *Br J Sports Med*, 43(13).
49. Loland, S. (2021). Classification in sport: a question of fairness. *Eur J Sport Sci*, 21(11).
50. Mann, D. L., et al. (2021). Classifying the evidence for evidence-based classification in Paralympic sport. *J Sports Sci*, 39(1).
51. McNamee, M., et al. (2021). Fairness, technology and the ethics of Paralympic sport classification. *Eur J Sport Sci*, 21(11).
52. IPC (2024). *IPC's classification code*. International Paralympic Committee.
53. Runciman, P., & Derman, W. (2018). Athletes with brain injury: pathophysiologic and medical challenges. *Phys Med Rehabil Clin N Am*, 29(2).
54. Frankel, H. L. (2012). The Sir Ludwig Guttmann Lecture 2012: the contribution of Stoke Mandeville Hospital to spinal cord injuries. *Spinal Cord*, 50(11).
55. Connick, M. J., et al. (2018). Evolution and development of best practice in Paralympic classification. In Brittain, I. Beacom, A. (Eds.) *The Palgrave handbook of paralympic studies*. Palgrave Macmillan.
56. Reina, R. (2014). Evidence-based classification in paralympic sport: application to football -7-a-Side. *Eur J Hum Mov*, 32.
57. Yanci, J., et al. (2019). Evaluation of the official match external load in soccer players with cerebral palsy. *J Strength Cond Res*, 33(3).
58. Henríquez, M., et al. (2023). Sex differences in change of direction deficit and asymmetries in footballers with cerebral palsy. *Scand J Med Sci Sports*, 33(8).
59. Roldan, A., et al. (2022). To what degree does limb spasticity affect motor performance in para-footballers with cerebral palsy? *Front Physiol*, 12.
60. Reina, R., et al. (2021). Is impaired coordination related to match physical load in footballers with cerebral palsy of different sport classes? *J Sports Sci*, 39(1).
61. Henríquez, M., et al. (2020). Physical demands of para-footballers with cerebral palsy in a small-sided game. *J Sports Med Phys Fitness*, 60(9).
62. Peña-González, I., et al. (2021). Change-of-direction ability of para-footballers with cerebral palsy under a new evidence-based and sport-specific classification system. *Int J Sports Physiol Perform*, 16(2).
63. Reina, R., et al. (2020). Evaluation of the bilateral function in para-athletes with spastic hemiplegia: a model-based clustering approach. *J Sci Med Sport*, 23(8).
64. Reina, R., et al. (2017). How does the ball influence the performance of change of direction and sprint tests in para-footballers with brain impairments? Implications for evidence-based classification in CP-Football. *PLoS One*, 12(11).
65. Yanci, J., et al. (2021). Performance analysis in football-specific tests by para-footballers with cerebral palsy: implications for evidence-based classification. *Int J Sports Physiol Perform*, 16(9).

66. Henríquez, M., et al. (2023). Contextual factors and match-physical performance of international-level footballers with cerebral palsy. *Sci Med Footb*, 33(8).
67. Reina, R., et al. (2020). Activity limitation and match load in para-footballers with cerebral palsy: an approach for evidence-based classification. *Scand J Med Sci Sports*, 30(3).
68. Tweedy, S. M., et al. (2018). Applying scientific principles to enhance Paralympic classification now and in the future: a research primer for rehabilitation specialists. *Phys Med Rehabil Clin N Am*, 29(2).
69. Henríquez, M., et al. (2021). Physical responses by cerebral palsy footballers in matches played at sea level and moderate altitude. *Res Sports Med*, 31(3).
70. Cammidge, S. A. (2017). *Consulting the sport community for the development of an evidence-based classification system in cerebral palsy football.* Miguel Herna´ndez University.
71. Reina, R., et al. (2018). Vertical and horizontal jump capacity in international cerebral palsy football players. *Int J Sports Physiol Perform*, 13(5).
72. Reina, R., et al. (2016). Change of direction ability performance in cerebral palsy football players according to functional profiles. *Front Physiol*, 6.
73. Roldan, A., et al. (2020). An observational tool to assess activity limitation in ambulatory people with cerebral palsy when performing motor skills. *Int J Environ Res Public Health*, 17(6).
74. Pastor, D., et al. (2019). A mathematical model for decision-making in the classification of para-footballers with different severity of coordination impairments. *J Sports Sci*, 37(12).
75. Sarabia, J. M., et al. (2021). Using decision trees to support classifiers' decision-making about activity limitation of cerebral palsy footballers. *Int J Environ Res Public Health*, 18(8).
76. Yanci, J., et al. (2018). External match loads of footballers with cerebral palsy: a comparison among sport classes. *Int J Sports Physiol Perform*, 13(5).
77. Teixeira J. E., et al. (2021). Effects of match location, quality of opposition and match outcome on match running performance in a Portuguese professional football team. *Entropy*, 23(8).
78. Hoppe, M. W., et al. (2018). Validity and reliability of GPS and LPS for measuring distances covered and sprint mechanical properties in team sports. *PLoS One*, 13(2).
79. Abbott, W., et al. (2018). Positional differences in GPS outputs and perceived exertion during soccer training games and competition. *J Strength Cond Res*, 32(11).
80. Yanci, J, et al. (2022). Comparison of the physical response during official matches and small-sided games in international cerebral palsy footballers: implications for evidence-based classification. *Adapt Phys Activ Q*, 40(1).
81. Peña-González, I., et al. (2021). Relationship between physical performance and match load and effects of two consecutive matches in cerebral palsy footballers. *Retos*, 41.
82. Achten, J., & Jeukendrup, A. E. (2003). Heart rate monitoring. *Sports Med*, 33(7).
83. Schneider, C., et al. (2018). Heart rate monitoring in team sports—a conceptual framework for contextualizing heart rate measures for training and recovery prescription. *Front Physiol*, 31(9).

84. Foster, C., et al. (2001). A new approach to monitoring exercise training. *J Strength Cond Res*, 15(1).
85. Goh, A. M. (2022). Global positioning system activity profile in male para footballers with cerebral palsy: does training meet the match-play intensity in a three-day national tournament? *Am J Phys Med Rehabil*, 101(12).
86. Sparks, M., et al. (2017). Internal and external match loads of university-level soccer players: a comparison between methods. *J Strength Cond Res*, 31(4).
87. de Freitas, V., et al. (2020). Internal training load and performance indices of cerebral palsy football players and effects of one week with and without training on heart rate variability. *J Phys Ed Sport*, 20.
88. Hewitt, A., et al. (2016). Game style in soccer: what is it and can we quantify it? *Int J Perf Anal Spor*, 16(1).
89. Peña-González, I., et al. (2023). Analysis of scored goals in the cerebral palsy football World Cup. *J Sports Sci*, 40(22).
90. Gamonales, J. M., et al. (2019). Sport performance indicators in Football 7-A-side for people with cerebral palsy. *Rev Int Med Cienc Ac*, 19(74).
91. Yanci, J. (2015). Analysis of goals scored by players with cerebral palsy in official football 7-a-side matches. *Kinesiology*, 47(2).
92. Díez, A., et al. (2021). Influence of contextual factors on physical demands and technical-tactical actions regarding playing position in professional soccer players. *BMC Sports Sci Med Rehabil*, 13(1).
93. Graham, H. K., et al. (2016). Cerebral palsy. *Nat Rev Dis Primers*, 2.
94. Goh, A. M., et al. (2023). Characteristics of goals scored in open play at the 2017 and 2018 Australian national cerebral palsy football championship. *Int J Spor Sci & Coach*, 18(3).
95. Gamonales, J. M., et al. (2023). Sport performance evolution of football 7-A-side for people with cerebral palsy: 2012–2016. *Rev Int Med Cienc Ac*, 23(89).
96. Errekagorri, I., et al. (2023). Performance analysis of the Spanish men's top and second professional football division teams during eight consecutive seasons. *Sensors*, 23(22).
97. Yanci, J., et al. (2016). Muscle strength and anaerobic performance in football players with cerebral palsy. *Disabil Health J*, 9(2).
98. Peña-González, I., & Moya-Ramón, M. (2023). Physical performance preparation for the cerebral palsy football world cup: a team study. *Apunts Sports Med*, 58(218).
99. Peña-González, I., et al. (2023). Changes in sprint force–velocity profile in international para footballers. *Int J Sports Physiol Perform*, 18(5).
100. Peña-González, I., et al. (2022). International football players with cerebral palsy maintained their physical fitness after a self-training program during the COVID-19 lockdown. *PeerJ*, 10.
101. Peña-González, I., et al. (2022). Assessing the sprint force-velocity profile in international football players with cerebral palsy: validity, reliability and sport class' profiles. *J Hum Kinet*, 82(1).
102. Morin, J. B., & Samozino, P. (2016). Interpreting power-force-velocity profiles for individualized and specific training. *Int J Sports Physiol Perform*, 11(2).
103. Daniel, L. F., et al. (2020). Validity and reliability of a test battery to assess change of directions with ball dribbling in para-footballers with cerebral palsy. *Brain Sci*, 10(2).

104. Duncan, M. J., et al. (2022). Perception of affordances for dribbling in soccer: exploring children as architects of skill development opportunity. *Sports*, 10(7).
105. Kloyiam, S., et al. (2011). Soccer-specific endurance and running economy in soccer players with cerebral palsy. *Adapt Phys Activ Q*, 28(4).
106. Yanci, J., et al. (2014). Jump capacity in cerebral palsy soccer players. *Rev Int Med Cienc Ac*, 14(54).
107. Coswig, V., et al. (2019). Assessing the validity of the MyJUMP2 app for measuring different jumps in professional cerebral palsy football players: an experimental study. *JMIR Mhealth Uhealth*, 7(1).
108. Fleeton, J. R., et al. (2020). Strength training to improve performance in athletes with cerebral palsy: a systematic review of current evidence. *J Strength Cond Res*, 34(6).
109. Gillett, J. G., et al. (2018). Functional anaerobic and strength training in young adults with cerebral palsy. *Med Sci Sports Exerc*, 50(8).
110. Scholtes V. A., et al. (2010). Effectiveness of functional progressive resistance exercise strength training on muscle strength and mobility in children with cerebral palsy: a randomized controlled trial. *Dev Med Child Neurol*, 52(6).
111. Taylor, N. F., Dodd, K. J., Baker, R. J., Willoughby, K., Thomason, P., & Graham, H. K. (2013). Progressive resistance training and mobility-related function in young people with cerebral palsy: a randomized controlled trial. *Dev Med Child Neurol*, 55(9), 806–812.
112. Moreau, N. G., et al. (2012). Rapid force generation is impaired in cerebral palsy and is related to decreased muscle size and functional mobility. *Gait Posture*, 35(1).
113. Alarcón, A., et al. (2021). Effects of lower limb eccentric strength training on functional measurements in football players with cerebral palsy. *EUJAPA*, 14(1).
114. Umar, F., et al. (2020). Increasing speed and agility of cerebral palsy football Indonesian player with UMAC-CPF exercise model. *Int J Hum Mov Spor Sci*, 8(6).
115. Jowett, S. (2007). Interdependence analysis and the 3 + 1Cs model in the coach-athlete relationship. In Jowett , S. Lavallee, D. (Eds.) *Social psychology in sport*. Human Kinetics.
116. Jowett, S. (2017). Coaching effectiveness: the coach–athlete relationship at its heart. *Curr Opin iPsychol*, 16.
117. Vella, S. A., et al. (2013). The relationship between coach leadership, the coach–athlete relationship, team success, and the positive developmental experiences of adolescent soccer players. *Phys Educ Sport Pedagogy*, 18.
118. Jowett, S., & Chaundy, V. (2004). An investigation into the impact of coach leadership and coach - athlete relationship on group cohesion. *Group Dyn Theor Res Prac*, 8.
119. Northouse, P. G. (2018). *Leadership: Theory and practice*. Sage Publications.
120. Chelladurai, P. (2012). Leadership and manifestations of sport. In Murphy, S. M. (Ed.) *Handbook of sport and performance psychology*. Oxford University Press.
121. Bass, B. M. (1985). *Leadership and Performance beyong expectations*. Free Press.
122. Fransen, K. (2021). El Poder del Liderazgo de Jugadores en Equipos Deportivos. In García-Calvo, T. Leo , F. M. Cervelló , E. (Eds.) *Dirección de equipos deportivos*. Tirant Humanidades.

123. Fransen, K., et al. (2020). The impact of identity leadership on team functioning and well-being in team sport: is psychological safety the missing link? *Psychol Sport Exerc*, 51.
124. Ames, C. (1992). Classrooms: goals, structures, and student motivation. *J Educ Psychol*, 84(3).
125. Ryan, R. M., & Deci, E. L. (2017). *Self-determination theory: basic psychological needs in motivation, development, and wellness*. Guilford Publications.
126. Carron, A. V., et al. (2002). Team cohesion and team success in sport. *J Sports Sci*, 20(2).
127. Leo, F. M., et al. (2022). Multilevel analysis of coach leadership, group cohesion and collective efficacy in semiprofessional football teams. *Int J Sport Psychol*, 53.
128. De Backer, M., et al. (2011). Do perceived justice and need support of the coach predict team identification and cohesion? Testing their relative importance among top volleyball and handball players in Belgium and Norway. *Psychol Sport Exerc*, 12.
129. García-Calvo, T., et al. (2019). Coach justice and competence in football. In *Football psychology: from theory to practice*. Routledge.
130. Bandura, A. (1997). *Self-efficacy: the exercise of control*. Macmillan.
131. Fransen, K., et al. (2012). "Yes, we can!": perceptions of collective efficacy sources in volleyball. *J Sports Sci*, 30.
132. Hampson, R., & Jowett, S. (2014). Effects of coach leadership and coach-athlete relationship on collective efficacy. *Scand J Med Sci Spor*, 24.
133. Jowett, S., & Shanmugam, V. (2016). Relational coaching in sport: its psychological underpinnings and practical effectiveness. In *Routledge international handbook of sport psychology*. Routledge.
134. Patel, D. R., et al. (2020). Cerebral palsy in children: a clinical overview. *Transl Pediatr*, 9(1).
135. Milligan, T. A. (2021). Epilepsy: a clinical overview. *Am J Med*, 134(7).
136. Pérez, I. F., et al. (2023). Risk factors and outcome of epilepsy in adults with cerebral palsy or intellectual disability. *Epilepsy Behav*, 147.
137. Kuntz, S., et al. (2023). Association between multiple sclerosis and epilepsy: a systematic review and meta-analysis. *Mult Scler Relat Disord*, 69.
138. Arntz, R., et al. (2013). Post-stroke epilepsy in young adults: a long-term follow-up study. *PLoS One*, 8(2).
139. Sahoo, S. K., & Fountain, N. B. (2004). Epilepsy in football players and other land-based contact or collision sport athletes: when can they participate, and is there an increased risk? *Curr Sports Med Rep*, 3(5).
140. Van Den Bongard, F., et al. (2020). Sport and physical activity in epilepsy: a systematic review. *Dtsch Arztebl Int*, 117.
141. Alexander, H. B., et al. (2020). Incidence of seizure exacerbation and injury related to football participation in people with epilepsy. *Epilepsy Behav*, 104.
142. Blackmore, A. M., et al. (2016). Prevalence of symptoms associated with respiratory illness in children and young people with cerebral palsy. *Dev Med Child Neurol*, 58(7).
143. Guzmán H., J. M., et al. (2021). Asma y broncoconstricción inducida por ejercicio en el deportista de resistencia: actualización en diagnostico y tratamiento. *Archivos de la sociedad chilena de Medicina Del Deporte*, 66(1).

144. Kwon, Y. H., & Lee, H. Y. (2015). Differences in respiratory pressure and pulmonary function among children with spastic diplegic and hemiplegic cerebral palsy in comparison with normal controls. *J Phys Ther Sci*, 27(2).
145. Aroojis, A., et al. (2021). Hip displacement in cerebral palsy: the role of surveillance. *Indian J Orthop*, 55(1).
146. Howard, J. J., et al. (2023). Hip surveillance and management of hip displacement in children with cerebral palsy: clinical and ethical dilemmas. *J Clin Med*, 12(4).
147. Heimer, C. Y. W., et al. (2022). The impact of hip dysplasia on CAM impingement. *J Pers Med*, 12(7).
148. Short, S. M., et al. (2021). Hip and groin injury prevention in elite athletes and team sport – current challenges and opportunities. *Int J Sports Phys Ther*, 16(1).
149. Gibson, N., et al. (2022). Australian hip surveillance guidelines at 10 years: new evidence and implementation. *J Pediatr Rehabil Med*, 15(1).
150. Haugen, T., et al. (2019). Sprint running: from fundamental mechanics to practice - a review. *Eur J Appl Physiol*, 119(6).
151. Chappell, A., et al. (2019). Running in people with cerebral palsy: a systematic review. *Physiother Theory Pract*, 35(1).
152. Almansoof, H. S., et al. (2023). Role of ankle dorsiflexion in sports performance and injury risk: anarrative review. *Electron J Gen Med*, 20(5).
153. Novak, I., et al. (2020). State of the evidence traffic lights 2019: systematic review of interventions for preventing and treating children with cerebral palsy. *Curr Neurol Neurosci Rep*, 20(2).
154. Alizadeh, S., et al. (2023). Resistance training induces improvements in range of motion: a systematic review and meta-analysis. *Sports Med*, 53(3).
155. Galletti, M., et al. (2024). Short-term reduction of ankle spasticity after surgical lengthening of the triceps surae in chronic post-stroke patients: a retrospective cohort study. *Front Neurol*, 15.
156. Derman, W., et al. (2018). High precompetition injury rate dominates the injury profile at the Rio 2016 Summer Paralympic Games: a prospective cohort study of 51 198 athlete days. *Br J Sports Med*, 52(1).
157. Willick, S. E., et al. (2013). The epidemiology of injuries at the London 2012 Paralympic Games. *Br J Sports Med*, 47(7).
158. Patatoukas, D., et al. (2011). Disability-related injuries in athletes with disabilities. *Folia Med*, 53(1).
159. Webborn, N., et al. (2016). The epidemiology of injuries in football at the London 2012 Paralympic games. *PM & R*, 8(6).
160. Owoeye, O. B. A., et al. (2020). Reducing injuries in Soccer (Football): an Umbrella review of best evidence across the epidemiological framework for prevention. *Sports Med - Open*, 6(1).
161. Marín-Fermín, T., et al. (2023). Acute Ankle Sprain in Elite Athletes. *Foot Ankle Clin*, 28(2).
162. Halabchi, F., & Hassabi, M. (2020). Acute ankle sprain in athletes: clinical aspects and algorithmic approach. *World J Orthop*, 11(12).
163. Schiftan, G. S., et al. (2015). The effectiveness of proprioceptive training in preventing ankle sprains in sporting populations: a systematic review and meta-analysis. *J Sci Med Sport*, 18(3).

164. Emery, C. A., & Pasanen, K. (2019). Current trends in sport injury prevention. *Best Pract Res Clin Rheumatol*, 33(1).
165. Kalema, R. N., et al. (2021). Sprinting biomechanics and hamstring injuries: is there a link? a literature review. *Sports*, 9(10).
166. Clijsen, R., et al. (2022). Local heat applications as a treatment of physical and functional parameters in acute and chronic musculoskeletal disorders or pain. *Arch Phys Med Rehabil*, 103(3).
167. Johnson, M. I., et al. (2022). Efficacy and safety of transcutaneous electrical nerve stimulation (TENS) for acute and chronic pain in adults: a systematic review and meta-analysis of 381 studies (the meta-TENS study). *BMJ Open*, 12(2).
168. Cobo-Vicente, et al. (2021). Neuromuscular electrical stimulation improves muscle strength, biomechanics of movement, and functional mobility in children with chronic neurological disorders: a systematic review and meta-analysis. *Phys Ther*, 101(10).
169. Fernández-De-Las-Peñas, C., et al. (2021). Is dry needling effective for the management of spasticity, pain, and motor function in post-stroke patients? A systematic review and meta-analysis. *Pain Med*, 22(1).
170. Salvador, A. F., et al. (2016). Bilateral muscle strength symmetry and performance are improved following walk training with restricted blood flow in an elite paralympic sprint runner: case study. *Phys Ther Sport*, 20.
171. FIFA. (2019). *Women's football member associations survey report*. Federation Internationale de Football Association.
172. Martínez-Lagunas, V., et al. (2014). Women's football: player characteristics and demands of the game. *J Sport Health Sci*, 3(4).
173. Kirkendall, D. T., & Krustrup, P. (2022). Studying professional and recreational female footballers: a bibliometric exercise. *Scand J Med Sci Sports*, 32(1).
174. IFCPF. (2020). *IFCPF competition rules*. International Federation of Cerebral Palsy Football.
175. Lee, J., et al. (2021). Disability incidence rates for men and women in 23 countries: evidence on health effects of gender inequality. *J Gerontol A Biol Sci Med Sci*, 76(2).
176. Jalayondeja, C., et al. (2016). Physical activity, self-esteem, and quality of life among people with physical disability. *Southeast Asian J Trop Med Public Health*, 47(3).
177. Fagher, K., et al. (2023). Optimising health equity through para sport. *Br J Sports Med*, 57(3).
178. Ascondo, J., et al. (2023). Analysis of the barriers and motives for practicing physical activity and sport for people with a disability: differences according to gender and type of disability. *Int J Environ Res Public Health*, 20(2).
179. Dean, N. A., et al. (2024). "It looks good on paper, but it was never meant to be real": mixed-gender events in the paralympic movement. *Adapt Phys Activ Q*, 41(2).
180. Verschuren, O., et al. (2013). Anaerobic performance in children with cerebral palsy compared to children with typical development. *Ped Phys Ther*, 25(4).
181. Romeo, D. M., (2016). Sex differences in cerebral palsy on neuromotor outcome: a critical review. *Dev Med Child Neurol*, 58(8).

182. Henríquez, M., et al. (2021). Time – motion characteristics and physiological responses of para-footballers with cerebral palsy in two small-sided games and a simulated game. *Adapt Phys Activ Q*, 38(2).

183. Beato, M., et al. (2024). Monitoring readiness to train and perform in female football: current evidence and recommendations for practitioners. *Int J Sports Physiol Perform*, 19(3).

Index

For Product Safety Concerns and Information please contact our EU representative GPSR@taylorandfrancis.com
Taylor & Francis Verlag GmbH, Kaufingerstraße 24, 80331 München, Germany

www.ingramcontent.com/pod-product-compliance
Lightning Source LLC
LaVergne TN
LVHW010926110826
845149LV00013B/2500

* 9 7 8 1 0 3 2 7 0 8 9 5 9 *